George Tugwell

On the Mountain

Being the Welsh experiences of Abraham Black and Jonas White, Esquires,

moralists, photographers, fishermen, and botanists

George Tugwell

On the Mountain
Being the Welsh experiences of Abraham Black and Jonas White, Esquires, moralists, photographers, fishermen, and botanists

ISBN/EAN: 9783337288792

Printed in Europe, USA, Canada, Australia, Japan

Cover: Foto ©Andreas Hilbeck / pixelio.de

More available books at **www.hansebooks.com**

ON THE MOUNTAIN:

BEING

THE WELSH EXPERIENCES

OF

ABRAHAM BLACK & JONAS WHITE, ESQUIRES,

Moralists, Photographers, Fishermen,
and Botanists.

BY THE
REV. GEORGE TUGWELL, M.A.

ORIEL COLL., OXON.

LONDON:
RICHARD BENTLEY, NEW BURLINGTON STREET,
Publisher in Ordinary to Her Majesty.
1862.

"THE MOUNTAYNE MEN LIVE LONGER MANY A YEARE
 THAN THOSE IN VALE, IN PLAYNE, IN MARISH SOYLE;
A LUSTIE HART, A CLEAN COMPLEXION CLERE,
 THEY HAVE, ON HILL THAT FOR HARD LIVING TOYLE."

PREFACE.

I should like this book to fall into the hands, chiefly, of those who know, or are intending to know, something of the mountain district which is the scene of the story; and, also, of those who have travelled, or are intending to travel in any district, whether level or mountainous, whether English or foreign.

Not that I have aimed at writing either a Guide-book, or a compendious "Art of Travel," but that I wished to suggest some few thoughts of the following sort, which, however obvious they are, are still not as common as they might be.

I should like to remind a reader or two, at the least, that all real knowledge is essentially cumulative and assimilative: that the pleasure and the good which a traveller takes out of any given district is always in strict proportion to the knowledge and the cultivation which he takes into it; that to travel truly is not to flit, ghost-like, emptily through empty space, but to gather, bee-like, from flower and weed alike, that sustenance for dark and wintry days which the great garden of Nature can yield abundantly to every worker; that no knowledge, however slight or superficial, is valueless: that no district need be unprolific,—no " moorland " hopelessly " dreary," —no " shore " utterly " barren."

If I have added a story it is because no natural scenery is perfect until it contains a human element; until to natural beauty and force are added the moral beauty and force of goodness and love and adoration. Even Paradise was not perfect until Adam, and Eve, entered in.

In plain words, to travel truly a man must not only walk and ride and run and climb, but must know and read and think and see and love and worship. And if, as I said, this is an obvious remark, it is also one which many travellers On the Mountain and elsewhere might carry out more thoroughly than they do, to their own great advantage and that of other people.

To my friend, the Rev. H. B. Scougall, many thanks are due for his clever watercolour drawings (enlargements of stereograms of mine), which are so great an ornament to this volume.

To my friend and fellow-traveller, the Rev. T. F. Ravenshaw, thanks are also due for the majority of the botanical notes which are incorporated in the book:

TO HIM,

IN MEMORY OF MANY PLEASANT DAYS

OF NOT UNPROLIFIC IDLENESS,

HAPPILY SPENT TOGETHER

ON THE MOUNTAIN,

THIS STORY IS AFFECTIONATELY INSCRIBED.

Ilfracombe, N. Devon,
  September 1862.

CONTENTS.

CHAPTER I.
Entirely Introductory, and somewhat Biographical 1

CHAPTER II.
"En r-r-route!" 21

CHAPTER III.
The Lake of the Pleasant Retreat . . 49

CHAPTER IV.
The Giant's Throne 79

CHAPTER V.
From Cader to Snowdon 96

CHAPTER VI.
Hawarden Grange 113

CHAPTER VII.
A Chance Guest 129

CHAPTER VIII.
Pen-y-Gwryd 143

CHAPTER IX.
Excursionizing 176

CHAPTER X.
The Friend in Need 199

CHAPTER XI.
A Night on Snowdon 217

CHAPTER XII.
Homewards and Home 251

ON THE MOUNTAIN.

CHAPTER I.

ENTIRELY INTRODUCTORY, AND SOMEWHAT BIOGRAPHICAL.

ABRAHAM BLACK and his sister Caroline are at breakfast—time 9 o'clock, or thereabouts—on a cool shining summer morning, towards the end of June.

Marscombe Cottage stands in a sunny sheltered angle of one of those far northern Devonshire Combes, which trend from the high bleak moorlands to the grey jagged seaboard, and the perpetual music of the vast and trackless Atlantic.

Half-way down the Combe, which has been

running seawards hitherto, the valley takes a sudden and brief turn to the west, and there, on the hill-side facing south, Abraham Black built his cottage some ten or fifteen years ago, a low gable-ended many-cornered house of native grey slate-rock, with quoins and porch of white sparkling Cornish granite. A terraced garden, always trimly kept, and blazing with flowers, many of them hothouse rarities in less favoured climates, descends with granite steps and facings to the clear brown trout-stream in the basin of the Combe—the famous Marscombe trout-stream—the special hobby and pride of its owner and preserver.

Happy is the fisherman whom Abraham Black delights to favour with a spring week's hearty hospitality! His basket is filled six days of the seven in the shortest of morning's work. Such noble rock-pools are there in that little Combe, such deep-rolling eddies under the flashing falls and the stately osmundas in the scarped water-worn rock! Such long clear rippling "runs" between the low golden furze-brakes, and the purple shining heather-beds! And such trout! black-backed, deep-sided, yellow-bellied, fire-spotted, rising to the fly from their deeps, sudden and earnest as lightning; and when they rise, woe be to that man whose hand is not of the lightest, and tackle of the trustiest in that his hour of need.

Eastward of the cottage is a sheltering wood of low weather-bent oaks; beyond the stream the tall square tower of Marscombe Church breaks the hill-line; and beyond, again, the eye loses itself in the dim purple outlines of the great moor.

Abraham Black is a wealthy man, wealthy, not by reason of vast possessions and limitless income, but wealthy in a truer sense of the word, as owning a house and establishment far below that which his income might warrant him in possessing. For which reason, after all his daily wants are abundantly supplied, he has a yearly surplus which a less generous man would either hoard or find a difficulty in expending. But we do not find that this small matter has ever perplexed the mind of our friend. The parson of Marscombe—a capital fisherman and a no less famous naturalist by the way—informs us that there is scarcely a poor person in his parish. In one way or another Mr. Black finds work for all who can or will work, and is good to those who cannot work: while those who can and will not work, invariably find out, in the course of a short time, that Marscombe is not a suitable place of abode for them, and depart to more or less favoured districts. The work to be done in the parish, arises chiefly from the fact, that Mr. Black is an "amateur farmer" on a tolerably extensive scale—as the neighbouring yeoman farmers would call him if they had ever heard the phrase—and unlike most amateurs, he does not find it a losing speculation.

He says he clears his expenses, provides his household with meat, milk, poultry, vegetables, and bread, and employs a considerable portion of the labouring population of his parish; and, therefore, although he does not lay by money, he justly thinks that his farming speculations pay. And he further informs us, that he owes his success to the fact of his being, in Devonshire, a Devonshire farmer.

He is totally opposed to the centralization theory, which would sow steam-engines broadcast, and root up every hedge-bank and stone-fence throughout the length and breadth of the land. He gave unpardonable offence to the magnates at the last Barnstaple Agricultural, by totally refusing to have anything whatever to do with the latest improvements in steam-ploughs. He ventured to doubt the possibility, in the present state of the parish roads, of getting their machinery within fifteen miles of his farm; and he stated, that even were it conveyed piecemeal into his Barton yard, no remunerative "strength" would carry it up even into his home field. Neither will he pull down his fences, although he is aware that they occupy an eighth portion of available pasture or arable land, because he thinks that the spring easterly and the autumnal westerly winds would destroy far more than an eighth portion of his live stock and crops, were it not for that unfarmer-like protection. But he does insist upon thrashing machines and light ploughs and carts, and his turnips are diligently hoed, and most of his fat beasts are stall-fed; and he is scrupulously careful of his Barton manure, the annual loss of which is the ruin of most Devonshire farms and farmers; and, on the whole, his example is very much to be, and very little is, imitated by the North Devon agriculturist.

Personally, our friend Abraham is of middle stature, thick-set and broad-chested, with short curling hair above a broad white forehead, and fair ruddy Saxon features. He is enduring and active, though not particularly energetic in outward manner. He is a firm friend, and, to use an essentially English phrase, a man on whom one can depend.

His sister Caroline is one of those wonderful little people whom every one makes a pet of, and of whom no one was ever heard to say an unkind word, partly, perhaps, because an unkind thought never yet entered her own head. She has golden brown hair, and a transparent sunny complexion, and grey eyes which are always lighting up with merry mischievous good nature, or glistening in the half-light of their shadowy eye-lash fringes, if there is any one or any thing that would be comforted, or understood, or cared for. She may be ten years younger than her brother, and has kept house for him for the last five years, ever since she was eighteen, when her mother (whom she had nursed long and tenderly) died, and left her to her brother's care, as being her only near relation then surviving.

Which things being so, it occurs to us that our friends must have completed their breakfast, and that *that* is the postman's knock, who is rather before his time, and who, with a cheerful " Good mornin', Mr. Black! mornin' to 'e, miss!" delivers his letters through the open window, and sets off again at a rapid, easy, elastic pace, as if determined to be before his time at every other house on his beat.

"Hm—ah," said Mr. Black, breaking envelope after envelope, and chiefly consigning them, as being farmering and trade advertisements of no particular value, to the waste basket. At last he becomes absorbed in a somewhat scrambling and illegible scrawl, which he finally lays down on the table with a meditative air, and looks out of the window as intently as people do, when the last thing they desire is to see anything of interest in that direction.

"Now, Abey," said his sister, "that's what I call provoking. Here am I, curious of course, and I've got no letters of my own, and you give me or the waste-basket (which is the same thing) all those stupid printers, and when you get a real letter you look out of window, and try to whistle your one tune —which I think is a great shame. Now, if you please, tell me all about it."

"Eh?" replied Mr. Black, not yet recovered from his imaginary wandering out of the window. "Yes, I think it may do. I will write and say so at once."

"What will do, you stupid child? How do *I* know it will do, unless you tell me?

Who's your letter from, and what's it all about? Quick!" with a little impatient tap of the tiniest foot in Devonshire.

"Why, my dear," said Mr. Black, at length awakening to a sense of his sister's enquiries, "it's a letter from my best of old friends, Jonas White. You remember Jonas, who was at school with me? Why, of course you do. Yes, to be sure, he was down here only two years ago, and caught more trout in a week than I could catch in a fortnight, and I don't consider myself a very bad fisherman."

"O yes," said Caroline, trying hard to keep down a little sudden flush which would come up into her cheeks, "and talked, I suppose I may say, more nonsense, and took more exercise in the way of flourishing about, in the house and out of it, in a week, than you do in a month. Yes, I remember Mr. White; and pray what has he got to say for himself now?"

"Why, he says he is going to take his month or six weeks' run in ten days' time, and wants me to go into Wales with him to fish, and photograph, and botanise, and generally enjoy oneself. Of course I couldn't go without you to make tea, and tie my flies (we shall want lots of coch-y-bonddus up there), and dry the plants, and, in fact, do every thing for me, as you only can do it, dear. And so I shall write to say that we will meet him at Ilfracombe on the last day of the month, and all go together. It will do capitally, I think—don't you?"

"Oh!" said Caroline, and the small foot began to work again, only more energetically than before, and she spoke very quickly, looking up from under her long sweeping eyelashes, "that's what you call a capital plan, is it, sir? How do you think I should enjoy myself nowhere in particular in North Wales, when you two big men were tramping about all day over perpendicular mountains, and deep to your elbows all night in unknown chemical messes? Don't you think you could tie your own flies and dry your own plants for once, Mr. Abey? I see how it is. You don't know what to do with me, and so you say I must come; but I've got a much more capital plan of my own. There's Amy Lee writes me about two letters a week, asking me to come up and stay with them in Staffordshire; and she said in her last letter that her aunt, Mrs. Maberly, is staying at Ilfracombe, and is going up about the end of next week to them. So you see when you go, I can go—only with her—and then, you know, I shall come back by the time that you will want me home again. Do you see?"

Abraham Black did not usually take impressions very rapidly, and he was rather astonished and somewhat perplexed at this speech of his sister's. However, he only said, after a minute's pause, "Well, dear, I'm sure it will be a great disappointment to me if you don't come, and I'm sure you would enjoy yourself and be taken great care of; but if you want to go and see the Lees, I suppose it must be so. Only I'll tell you what," (brightening up as he went on,) "when you have been there some time, and we are settled down in Wales, I'll take a run into Staffordshire, and come and fetch you myself, and then we'll show you all the Welsh lions comfortably, and go home again together."

" Ah," said Caroline, looking half penitent, half mischievously provoking, " we shall see. Now you write your letters and settle it all, and I must go and see about dinner, or old Martha will be cross with me for a week."

So she departed, giving her brother a little kiss on his forehead as she went, and leaving behind with him the impression that he would almost rather not go to Wales at all, if she were not to go with him.

" But she will come afterwards, of course," he added to himself; and then, "I wonder why she wants to go and see Amy Lee at this particular time. I should have thought that the autumn would have done just as well."

So Jonas White got his letter. They were about to start together from Ilfracombe on the last day of June, as he proposed; and the rest of the three pages (for Abraham's letters were always short and practical, and moreover very legible, and in all respects a model much repudiated by Jonas) was filled with suggestions about fishing-tackle, botanical paper, (no presses to be used, only drying paper cut to the shape of a leather case, which fitted into the bottom of the portmanteau,) and photographic arrangements. " I think," he wrote, " we had better confine ourselves to stereoscopic work, as being a more portable amusement, and giving more effect in rock and mountain scenery. Just the cameras, dark slides, &c., and sufficient chemicals to prepare and develop in a dark room. I'll bring a big box large enough to hold all we want, and chemicals for both, so don't trouble yourself with any more preparations than just looking over your camera and legs."* A delicate piece of forethought on Abraham's

---

* The uninitiated and non-photographic reader must be informed that the "legs" referred to here, are not Jonas', strictly speaking, but the three outstretching legs of his camera-stand, which give that useful instrument (when seen at a distance) the appearance of some gigantic and feeble-minded spider, vainly endeavouring to hide itself in the rocks or the bushes which it is, in fact, depicting.

part, who knew that his friend's means were as limited as his heart was large. No allusion was made to Caroline by Abraham (a practical man) since she was not going with them, and he could not affirm that she would join them afterwards; and as Jonas never imagined for an instant that she was to be of the party, *he*, at all events was not disappointed.

Jonas White was, personally, vast—broad-shouldered, broad-chested, deep-voiced, large limbed, tall, lithe, active—a man who must be moving, when moving was in any way possible—a man who loved a stone wall, not as Abraham did because it was a good sort of fence, but because it was an obstacle to be moved, leapt, climbed. Mentally he was enthusiastic, metaphorical, imaginative, neither dogmatic nor addicted to argument, but rather introspective and self-contained, yet blazing out into rhetoric and declamation when he knew and liked his audience. He was fond of books, and retirement, and thought; fond of exercise, motion, and life—a strange seeming contradiction—a man whose earlier years might have rusted and cankered in the idleness of prosperity, a man whom work and adversity polished and fashioned to noble ends.

His history was not altogether a happy one, although he was altogether a happy man. His father had been the head partner in a large London firm, was a man of great wealth, possessed his town house and his country house, and enjoyed every luxury which he could desire, and which money could buy him. But one dreadful morning the great railway panic burst over the City like a hurricane, unexpectedly and fatally, and Mr. White's house fell, like so many others, without the chance of a struggle. In the process of time, however, it appeared that their ruin was not so utter as they had at first supposed, and at the expense of the private fortunes of all the partners, they paid eventually a dividend of twenty shillings in the pound. But the shock and the dread of the poverty to come, was too much for Mr. White, already enfeebled by long and anxious attention to business, and before his affairs were altogether wound up he died, leaving a widow, one daughter, and his only son Jonas, to fight out the battle of life together as best they could.

Here then came the decisive point in the life of Jonas White, one of those crises of which one generally occurs in the life of every man, when he either "does" and lives afterwards socially and morally, or "does not" and becomes a social cipher and a moral corpse. But Jonas, volatile, excitable, enthusiastic, romantic,* as he was, was not the man to

---

* I do not use this word in the secondary and evil sense to which it is relegated by the £ s. d. minds of the present period. Let me direct the reader's attention to the following extract from Richardson:—" ROMANCE, s. 'The Latin tongue ceased to be spoken in France about the 9th century, and was succeeded by what was called the Romance tongue, a mixture of the language of the Franks and bad Latin. As the songs of chivalry became the most popular compositions in that language, they were emphatically called Romans or Romants.'—*Percy.* As the old Romances were remarkable for the extravagance of their fictions, Romance became applicable to any wild extravagant story or invention of the imagination." Therefore the primary meaning of romantic is *chivalrous* in the full and best sense of that pregnant and good word.

cower under any storm that opposed his progress: it rather nerved and stimulated his impressionable nature. In the days of his father's prosperity he was brought up to no profession, for he needed none in a pecuniary point of view, and he was never idle for lack of interest or employment.

He had been passionately fond of plants and animals from his boyhood, and his rooms at Ashburton Court and in their house in town, were museums in all but tidiness. Endless cases of stuffed birds and beasts; aquaria, in which fresh water beetles and snails gazed through their glassy prisons at many-hued sea-anemones and peripatetic star-fish; cabinets of shells, of minerals, of fossils; folios of dried plants; Wardian cases of British and exotic ferns; shelves of huge books with hard names thereunto appertaining; cameras, microscopes, fishing rods, hammers, nets, and etceteras without end, were strewn about in every direction: and he was a bold and a skilful man who succeeded in paying the owner of all this property a morning visit

c

without effecting some unlucky breakage or losing himself in the labyrinth by which he was encompassed. Young as Jonas White was he had obtained no inconsiderable reputation in the scientific world, and was on the point of sailing for South America, as naturalist to an expedition then fitting out under Government, when the fatal crash came by which he and his family were brought at once to the verge of want. But he met his trouble as a man would meet it: he gave up his appointment for the sake of his mother and sister whom he would not leave in their sorrow: he sold almost all his books and instruments, reserving but a very few, and them only as memorials of old times; and he accepted the first situation that offered itself, that of junior clerk in a Bank not far from his late father's offices.

Mrs. White and her children lived in the smallest of lodgings in a new Paddington Terrace, and saved enough from the ruin to live there, with the help which Jonas brought in to the common stock from his small salary, and his endless abundance of cheerfulness and happy temperament.

"I wish, my dear Jonas," said Mrs. White, one day, "you would try and find out who it is that sends us this £100 cheque every Christmas morning. This is the third; and they all have been sent with the same note, 'from a friend who owed Mr. White more than he can now repay.' It is very strange, and I don't half like spending the money—I wish we knew how to return it."

"Well, mother," said Jonas, "you know as much about it as I do. I suppose that if it is a debt, the sender feels as much pleasure in paying as we do in receiving the money. And you know that without it we could not have paid the last doctor's bill for poor Sissy there, and so I think we had better spend it thankfully, and trust that the sender may long continue to owe us the annual remittance."

Which mystery, though then unsolvable, was solved at last.

But we must return to Jonas' letter from his friend Abraham Black, of which this same mystery reminds us, for, curiously enough, shortly before the Welsh tour entered into the mind of Jonas White, he had received a cheque for £50 from the same unknown hand, with merely a line enclosed to say that it was convenient to pay at that time this small instalment of the debt. So he made his arrangements with a light heart and a full purse, and settled that his mother and sister should take their holiday at the sea-side whilst he and Abraham rambled northwards in search of that health and enjoyment which a wandering on the mountain will so surely afford.

The ten days soon came to an end: camera, note-books, fishing tackle, strong and not new clothes and shoes, were duly collected and packed, and with something of his old love of excitement and enterprise Jonas White found himself whirling down West, and felt that the steady sweep of the early express was momentarily increasing the distance between himself and his daily work and his daily cares.

CHAPTER II.

"EN R-R-ROUTE!"

CAROLINE BLACK is gone into Staffordshire. Up to the very last moment her brother could not get her to promise that she would join them in Wales. No—she knew that Amy Lee would not spare her—she would meet her brother at Shrewsbury, perhaps,—she was not sure of that—perhaps Amy would come back into Devonshire with her—she would see. And all that Abraham could do was to assure her that he intended to fetch her in three weeks' time, and that then she must come—which of course she promptly and decidedly refused to do. And so the matter rested, Abraham's perplexity being vast and hopeless of a solution.

Abraham and Jonas spent a day and night at Ilfracombe before their departure, planning and chemicalizing. We shall not describe Ilfracombe, for our travellers' note-books do not describe it, and the broken fantastic outlines of its breezy hills, its dry clear invigorating atmosphere, the perpetual light and music of its pure Atlantic-born sea, all these are well-known and well-loved by those who best can care for the beauty of natural form and unsullied freshness. But we must make some record of the talk photographic which preceded their brief channel voyage, for in these photographic days there are few readers who have not some small interest in the matter, and very many we believe would not be unwilling to follow the example of our two wandering friends, and to bring back as the result of some similar ramble, some similar reminiscences.

Said Abraham Black, "I am just beginning to feel my responsibilities."

"And as how, and on what points?"

"Why, you have left all photographic

details to my decision, and there is the big box and there are the chemicals, and it is too late to make any other arrangements than those which I have made."

"And what may they be?"

"I know that all processes are much the same to you, Jonas, who contrive, rather inexplicably to me, to succeed in all."

"Now, Abraham, if you please—"

"Well then—I'll spare you—and tell you what I have done for us both. Of course nothing but a dry* process will satisfy us, for to say nothing of the resultant portability, the softness and detail of 'Fothergill' would alone make our choice one of necessity."

"Quite so—and so I suppose we must prepare some six dozen plates apiece this even-

---

* In a "dry process" the plates may be prepared some days or weeks before they are to be used—when dry they are "exposed" in the camera, and developed on the return from an expedition. No tent or heavy apparatus is therefore needed in the field, which when wet collodion is used must always be the case.

ing, and develop them on our return to Devonshire, trusting in our luck for six dozen resultant printable negatives—which on the whole is not a hopeful prospect."

"No—that's just where I have done what most photographic travellers don't do. I know people say that they have prepared four dozen plates and brought back four dozen good negatives after a month's excursion, and they may do so, but then they mayn't. A single error or piece of bad luck in the preparation may ruin, and has ruined the hopes of the best operator. Now I propose to reduce the matter to a certainty."

"Which is a much more hopeful prospect. But I don't quite see how, though."

"Why here's the big box—you see it's rather enormous, and I am afraid it weighs over 150 lbs., but besides all the requisite chemicals and apparatus it holds my dark tent, which the Marscombe village boys have already surnamed "Judy," from its likeness to the mysterious exterior of a peripatetic Punch-and-Judy show which lately pervaded our village. In this, the wet process is carried on publicly to the intense bewilderment of the rural mind, and it will serve for an operating room on our travels, whenever we cannot persuade a too-confiding landlady that a bed-room with a yellow blind is specially and peculiarly adapted for a photographic establishment. Thus we shall be able to prepare our plates *en route*, and develop them on the evening after exposure, so that we shall never leave a station without making sure of possessing good pictures thereof. Do you approve?"

"Utterly. Next to the possession of a live photographic van, *à la* Fenton, comes your plan. And my experience teaches me that, though prepared plates will keep, the less they are kept the better are the results. So *vivant* "Judy" and her travelling mausoleum, and may the Welsh mind appreciate her points, and the Welsh natives handle her as if they loved her. And now for a dozen plates apiece, and a pipe or so apiece, and then to bed; and here's wishing a calm sea and a '*bon voyage*' to-morrow morning."

Sounds of deglutition ensue, and no heel-taps; after which collodion and tobacco are very much in the ascendant, and the other lodgers proportionally and perhaps naturally indignant and expostulatory.

It is "a shining heavenly morning," this last day of June, as our travellers hurry down the grey pier at the mouth of the little Ilfracombe harbour, and embark themselves and their chattels on board the broad black clumsy passenger-boat which is to convey them to the steamer, already panting and plunging ominously in the wash of the tide beyond Lantern Hill. There is a narrow line of white surf girding the base of Hillsborough; there is a network of twisted cirri high in air, sweeping eastwards rapidly and continuously; now and then a huge mass of soft translucent cumulus rolls up over the green slopes of Slade Down, its crests glittering in the morning sun, and throwing a wide flying shadow over hill and valley as it travels onward; there are white-crested waves leaping and breaking far away in mid channel, flickering points of light on the moving trackless plain.

Jonas (dubiously). "A beautiful morning after last night's rain!"

Abraham (who is a good sailor). "Charming! I see there is quite a fresh breeze out in the channel, and a trifle of ground sea running too. We shall have a cool and pleasant passage, though not so rapid a one as we should have had if the wind had been more from the South'ard."

Jonas. "Ah! Indeed!"

By this time they are on board the steamer, which still continues to roll, and pitch, and plunge at her anchors, and sends out wreathing coils of inky smoke from her chimneys, and white fleecy steam clouds from her steam pipe, and rings her flapping jangling bell, and screams incoherently with her brazen steam-whistle, and altogether behaves in an irritable and generally disagreeable manner.

Jonas walks the deck, partly with the design of discovering what the binnacle is, of which marine object he has read, and is not sure whether it is a portion of the machinery of the vessel, or of her rigging; and partly with the design of getting his sea-legs into order by a little prefatory practice.

Abraham smokes calmly and happily beneath the shadow of "Judy," and muses of negatives.

At length the last unfortunate sheep is hoisted up the rocking plank, and imbecilly bleating, is kicked, and pushed, and prodded into its impromptu pen; the last passenger, an iron-grey man, with tight-fitting clothes, and no expression whatever in his prominent eyes, is on board; a complaining female, who appears to be a friend of the stewardess, and has no bonnet and a toothache, and is afraid she will be taken to Swansea against her will, is sent back in the sheep-boat, complaining as she goes; and then the anchor grinds slowly up, and the bell jangles, and the silent engines wake up to life, and the great paddle-wheels churn round in the frothy sea, and there is a waving of handkerchiefs from the Lantern Hill, and one sob from a pale sickly-looking woman with a baby in her arms, who never looks up, and seems past active care— and so they are off.

Very much to the relief of Jonas, for the ground sea is in reality trifling, and the vessel freed from the irritating bonds of her anchorage glides away pleasantly enough through the white chopping sea, and that dull heavy vibration of every timber in answer to the pulsation of the engines is, we all know, nothing,—when we are used to it.

The sister peaks of the seven Torrs, and the grey scarp of Hillsborough, and the purple heights of Hangman begin to recede; there open out the iron precipices of Harty Point, and the wild ocean granite-peak of Lundy. The barred and flecked cirri are gone, and the sun shines out fervently. Moreover, in mid-channel the Atlantic rollers are certainly observable, and the vessel pitches and rolls over them in a noticable manner.

The iron-grey man with the tight clothes and the prominent expressionless eyes has a theory on the subject of that "*maladie de mer* " which is so disagreeable on these otherwise agreeable occasions ; he becomes for the time peripatetic, awfully and wonderfully peripatetic. He selects two points, invisible to other eyes than his own, on the deck of the vessel ; he extracts with a sudden snap a newspaper from beneath his arm, and then oscillates eternally between these points, reading as he goes. The more the vessel rolls the faster he walks, and the harder he reads. He performs the most marvellous gymnastic feats with his legs—all with his legs, for he is ironly immovable from his pelvis upwards—in order to preserve his balance, which he does preserve in a way totally unaccountable to Jonas, who is extended feebly on a pile of wraps, and wishes the iron-grey man would be ill at once and have done with it. But he is not ill, and performs further astounding feats in the development of his peripatetic theory; he jerks out a pile of stiffly-folded letters from a rigid pocket-book ; he extracts them from their envelopes one by one, the vessel rolling from crescendo up to fortissimo ;

he reads them one by one; he replaces them one by one in the rigid book; and then he proceeds with his ambulatory newspaper, still oscillating eternally between his extreme points as he reads.

Jonas closes his eyes in despair, and sees no more.

There is another theorist on board, who is less fortunate than the iron-grey man. He has ascertained by mathematical calculation, that the centre of the ship's gravity is situated somewhere between the paddle-wheels, and that consequently there will be less oscillation in that part than in any other; and he knows, moreover, that sea-sickness arises from spasms of the diaphragm—diaphragm influenced by voluntary muscles—muscles affected by nerves communicating with the brain—brain stimulated through the retina and its optic nerve, which are abnormally excited by the absence of that stability to which they are accustomed. Well-armed with which theory, physical and anatomical, he grasps firmly the shining balustrades of the iron-bound stairs which lead to the captain's bridge between the paddle-boxes, and fixes his eye steadily on the cap of the foremast. Ably argued and bravely executed, O grey-haired and seedy-coated philosopher! whose theory deserves a better fate—for before the Mumbles are sighted, he and Jonas are fellow-sufferers, and with the finger of tenderness we draw the veil of obscurity over the kindred agonies which remorselessly ensue.

Swansea at last! Past the white lighthouse shaft—past an iron American clipper in the roads, whose squared yards and tapering spars stand out against the sky like a good photograph, as Abraham observes (Jonas observes nothing)—past groups of trim villas on a low grassy height—then gliding smoothly into a tidal estuary through rows of skeleton piles and flood-gates; and so the voyage is over.

Jonas. "O, Abraham, do look after "Judy;" I can't!"

"Judy," at that instant, is, with all her ten-stone weight, on the shoulders of a vast, light-limbed, crisp-haired, sun-burnt son of Anak, who is executing a tight-rope dance with his burden on the ship's gunwale, and finally lands it on the quay as lightly as though it had been a band-box, or a millinor's assortment of latest crinoline.

Then there is a rush of rail along a low sandy shore, where shallow glittering estuaries run up continuously into the land like white soft fingers of a gigantic hand.

So into Carmarthen—dullest and most patient-looking of country places.

Abraham. "Jonas, what do you think of the Welsh, regarding them in the light of a nation of colourists?"

Jonas (who is much better, and begins to look at the ocean again from an artistic and poetical point of view). "Eh? Do you allude to those black old women with steeple-hats and no-coloured neckerchiefs?"

Abraham. "No; but the houses."

Jonas. "Ah! Intensely refreshing! First a bright salmon-coloured house, with a dash of blue or white about the windows; then a very yellow house; then a very white house with a black door; then purple Bangor-slating; then a patch of vivid green on shutter or gateway. Crude on the whole, and sinning hugely now and then against the theory of complementation, but nevertheless, as an aboriginal expression of colour-feeling, intensely refreshing, and that especially so to me after my experiences of dingy London suburbs, and cold-grey Devonshire villages."

Abraham. "I wonder why the English are nationally obtuse on the subject of colour, and reject all pure colour with a persevering unanimity? I wonder why they use brick, not because it is red, but because it happens to be a convenient form of buildable clay baked fortuitously into that pigmental result? I wonder why men consider that the universal use of whitewash is justifiable because it is cleanly, procurable, economical?"

Jonas. "I wonder why a lobster turns red when he is boiled, don't you? How can I tell? Look you—there are two brief facts annotated by my experience: one, that nine men out of ten would fail miserably were they to attempt the choosing of a paper which was to suit a given carpet, or a given set of curtains; would fail too, very probably, in buying a neck-tie, or a ribbon for their straw-hats, which should agree with the rest of their clothing: and that forty-nine men out of fifty could not match with any reliable accuracy half-a-dozen different shades of wool at a 'Berlin Repository.' Fact the second, is this; that five women out of ten (the whole ten being grossly ignorant of colour theories whether of Chevreul, Hay, Field, or Gardner Wilkinson) will dress themselves in perfect conformity with the laws of colour; will carpet and paper and curtain their drawing-rooms with more or less success; and the whole ten will match shades of silk or wool with almost invariable certainty. The why of which I take to be thought, practice, observation. A woman naturally wishes to be dressed well, to be surrounded with objects which are both objectively and subjectively beautiful—that is, which are both pretty and becoming.

She has time to think about the matter; and so she thinks; and so she succeeds.

"Women educate their sense of colour; men don't, as a rule: perhaps because they have little time, and less natural inclination than women for such things: perhaps because, unfortunately, it is not the custom for men to be so educated.

"This of men as contrasted with women: but your question deals with the fact that some groups of men are better colourists than other groups."

Abraham (in the intervals of his matutinal pipe). "Quite so. You believe in the fact, don't you?"

Jonas. "I can't help doing so: but it is not easy to account for it. One would say, of course, at first, that local influences accounted for the matter: that in tropical climates where vegetation, plumage, and so forth, are varied and bright coloured, the eye is habituated to the perception of varied and bright colours: that the Turk wears his fez, the Pyrenean his scarlet sash, the Persian his coloured raiment, because 'the trailers on the crag,' the dry-throated cicala, and the vast-winged butterfly, are radiant, gorgeous, jewel hued; and so that here in grey and rainy England men affect sombre tints and the absence of pure colour, because the sky is gloomy, and the hill-sides veiled in mist.

"But then crops out this disturbing fact, that on two sides of the narrow channel which we have just crossed, in two districts where almost the same natural influences prevail, we find so vast a difference as that afforded by the many-coloured towns of Swansea and Carmarthen, and the grey-tinted Devonshire village of Marscombe."

Abraham. "Well, I think that your theory of local influence is the true one, and only fails you because you don't carry it far enough. In Devonshire the native stone is grey slate, and a brick-field is unknown. Here bright-yellow bricks are a product of the district—hereabouts purple slating may be hewn out of the rock—here, or rather at Swansea, a no small place of commercial enterprise, they import largely yellow ochre, red lead, and what not. The local influence is one of bright colour, and so the people become accustomed to colour, and once accustomed to it the eye can never be satisfied without its spread and continuance."

Jonas. "Ah, I see. I didn't think of that, and feel happier; for from my youth up I have been afflicted with the why-why malady, and seeking many reasons find but few. We will have another colour chat another time, for the horses are coming out of the yard, and "Judy's" fate is hanging on the balance of a diminutive and irascible Welshman, who jabbers violently in inarticulate Welsh, and swears volubly in broken English—a fact I have noticed before, and one which speaks volumes in favour of the primitive morality of the Cymry."

One might write an immense and absorbingly erudite work in four volumes octavo, calf-lettered, on the subject of Public conveyances: commencing of course with Noah's Ark, whose object was to do as little distance as possible in a given space of time, and ending (after the lapse of a few years) with the night express on the Paris and Pekin Grand Junction, whose object will be very much the reverse. Moreover it is evident that the poetical episode in the great work-to-be (in spite of the golden-fleeced Argo, the jewelled castle-bearing elephant, the merry Irish jaunting-car with its ringing laughter and its flashing eyes) must be the chapter or chapters on stage-coaches.

Even in these crashing, rushing locomotive days of ours, days of the reign of Iron the King, and Undine his subtle-minded, all-powerful Water-Queen, there remains no small affection for the crawling time-eating mode of progression extant in our great-grandfathers' middle-ages. And the reason (as Jonas remarks ably enough in his very illegible diary) for this strange unpractical sympathy which still lingers in the heart of the most practical nation under the sun, arises from the influence of the human element which surrounded the old stage-coach and which deserts the modern railway-train. A traveller in former days had time and opportunity for sympathy with his travelling kind, which now he has not. Moreover the sympathy was not an objectless diffusive twilight, it radiated as noonday sunlight from a common centre. The many-coated, abnormal-gloved, brandies-and-water absorbing coachman had a personal individual interest in every human belonging of his coach, from the portly Squire of broad acres on the box, to Jim the shirtless and parentless whose life-mission was to see that the kicking-straps of Beeswing were properly adjusted, before she left the Lion Yard, the last of the team, with ears well back and a quick-handed helper on either side.

And this Phaetonical sympathy was in a manner reciprocal. At school one used to like Phaeton because he evidently had some "go" in him, and one was inclined to overlook that little *faux pas* of his, whereby he played the Pluto in the Jovian regions. In coaching days one rather took to the coachman, (although he evidently took too much to alcohol, and winked unnecessarily at unnecessarily be-ribboned barmaids,) partly because he was like the Czar, a highway autocrat, and partly because he was an undeniable whip, Beeswing hadn't a chance with him, and he would pull up his team of "three blind 'uns and a bolter" at the Golden Lion, Bloomsbury, after their fourteen mile gallop from the King's Arms, Tadcaster, to all appearance as fresh and as lively as if their heads were turned accidentally in the wrong direction, and the Tadcaster ostlers were to see their faces again in a short hour's time.

Now-a-days a railway guard is a guard to the traveller, and nothing more to him; an engine-driver is a part of the machine; a fellow traveller is rather in the way than not, for one can't put one's legs up in consequence, and one has little time and no silence for conversation.

But agreeable and sympathetic as stage-coach travelling may have been, perhaps is, ou a level line of road with a clear sky overhead, and the steady long-swinging gallop of four three-quarters bred well-seasoned roadsters for locomotive power; it is quite another thing when the horses are Welsh horses, the roads Welsh mid-country roads (we do not speak of Telford's magnificently engineered mountain-highway), and the sky a Welsh sky, a varied and picturesque diorama of cloud, rain, mist, and wind.

Jonas and Abraham indeed needed much consolation, poetical, sympathetic, historical, and what not, for the road was as bad as it could be, and the weather, if possible, worse.

There is on the top of a coach a region unknown to the ordinary well-drest tourist, who luxuriates in the neighbourhood of the shilling-loving Jehu. This is a back slum, a threepenny night-garret under gaping tiles, in truth a hard-seated narrow-benched purgatory at the end of all things coachy, dedicated to travelling ammoniacal ostlers, mal-odorous, damp-bundled peasants, and the like.

Hither by the Welsh Parca steeple-crowned and implacable, were relegated Abraham Black and Jonas White, together with five other unfortunates, apparently because the moving purgatory was only capable of torturing four people at a time with any bearable amount of agony.

There was a short, thick, white-handed, black-haired, hunch-backed, Welsh parson, amiable and enduring, "but bandy." There was his wife, clear pink-and-white complexioned, and tempered as angels are, or ought to be. There were his and her two children aged three and nothing respectively. There was a tall, plump, soft-fleshed, big-boned, Welsh nurse, in a cotton print, and a faded tulle bonnet of her mistress', trimmed with faded delicately-made flowers, and mingling quaintly with her own wiry unkempt black hair. There was a youth bound to a hitherto undiscovered Welsh village, who for his sins suffered in silence, and probably walked to his mountain bourne on a future and wiser occasion.

For it rained cats and dogs, Welsh goats, trumpeting mountain bulls, and other animals. The parson's wife put up a tattered umbrella, which, so far as it was capable of conducting anything anywhere, conducted streams of puce-coloured fluid down the neck and into the coat-pocket (where he kept cigar-lights and a well-bound note-book) of the patient Abraham. At intervals of ten minutes the Welsh Bonne fed the child aged nothing with a dubious liquid out of an ancient and fish-like soda-water bottle, and further regaled It with amorphous masses of what might have been bread or cake once, and then was'nt. It was naturally, and obviously, ill in consequence: It screamed: It's sister (or brother) screamed sympathetically : It's nurse in her attempts to calm the new-born tempest capsized the soda-water bottle into the shirt-front of Jonas, and trod violently on his sensitive and London-made boot. Jonas waxed wrath and rhetorical, the children yelled and howled, the women were at their wits' end, the parson smiled blandly, the rain fell, and the wind blew, and the coach rocked, and swerved, and plashed along the hilly roads—and so they arrived at Lampeter.

Lampeter, to them, was a wide street of white houses, pervaded by ill-drest youths in cornerless college caps, and infested by a tuneless sore-throated brass-band trumpeting feebly in cataracts of rain.

The whole country from Carmarthen to Aber-eyron*—a tiny village down in the flats by the sea, and remarkable for a well-restored decorated church, with a good broach-spire appertaining—is, when visible, strictly a transitional district. Here are boulder-built hovels surrounded by desolate moor, where the cotton-grass streamers flaunt in the flying wind. Here is a lawn-shaven, elm-shadowed park enclosure, and the sleek-hided black Welsh cattle feed leisurely within sight of the drawing-room windows of the well-to-do 'Squire Owen-ap-Jones-ap-Rice-ap-Caradoc-ap-

---

* *Lavatera arborea* (Tree mallow) grows here luxuriantly; also *Silene maritima* distinguished from *S. inflata*, which it much resembles, in that the petals are crowned, and that the barren procumbent shoots result in a cushion-like form.

――Davy Jones alone can finish the catalogue in the lapse of briny ages.

From Aber-eyron onwards are Devonian rounded cliffs and downs of out-cropping, grey-weathered slate; flat stretches of alluvial pasturage wandering down to white sands and black reefs of sea-weed-wreathed rocks— and then come, welcome change, the shining sea-mirrored terraces of Aberystwith.

Aberystwith is a bright stretch of white houses on a bank of many-coloured pebbles, and pebbly sand, with a green clear breezy sea beyond, and a fresh clear invigorating atmosphere around. A place where a worn-out man may do nothing (in fact there is nothing to do) for days, and be cured by means of his sea-born indolence—a place where Abraham photographed the only photographable object in the neighbourhood, the adjoined castle ruins situated on a swelling promontory between the old town on the Ystwith, and the new town on the sea.

On the undulating ruin-crowned banks in the vicinity of the castle, Jonas found and pounced upon as a prize, the strawberry trefoil (*Trifolium fragiferum*) with its pretty rose-coloured blossoms, and its heart-shaped leaves. The dry sea-banks to the right of the town were radiant with the yellow flowers of the horned poppy (*Glaucium luteum*): there too were straggling crowns of buck's-horn plantain (*Plantago Coronopus*), beds of the rose-coloured *Geranium molle*, and the tiny pale-red petals of the sea-storks-bill (*Erodium maritimum*): and every weather-beaten lichen-covered cottage roof was ablaze with the yellow bloom of the common stone-crop (*Sedum acre*), or was fringed with the less common *S. reflexum*, whose pendant shoots hung candelabra-like in graceful wind-rocked wreaths and festoons. So that Jonas, not indeed thinking that all his gatherings were prizes, but gathering many and admiring all for their delicate beauty and their perfect colouring, was well satisfied with his morning's botanizing, and departed radiantly on a clear shining morning, and a roomy coach-top northward and northward still, for Pen-y-gwryd is far away on the high mountains, and holiday-time stayeth its rapid course for no holiday-making man.

And a lovely drive is that drive northwards from Aberystwith. There are wooded hills, multitudinous as Welsh woods are in colour and foliage; glimpses of the blue distant sea; clear brown mountain streams; and the great Cader Idris, with his black blunted peak far-off and cloud-crowned. Then comes the clean white street of Machynlleth, loved by fishermen, and artist men; then a steep Pyrenean mountain-gorge, with wind-rolling woods on scarped sides, and a flashing stream in the valley below, climbs up to the very foot of Cader; and there lies Llyn Mwyngyl, the beautiful, the big-trout-haunted, the "Lake of the Pleasant Retreat," bright and sparkling, and clear-watered, opalescent in its changeful radiance, beneath the flitting shadows of the great Giant's rocky Throne.

THE LAKE OF THE PLEASANT RETREAT

CHAPTER III.

THE LAKE OF THE PLEASANT RETREAT.

OF all "pleasant retreats" wherein to enjoy a week's calm idleness—say a fortnight's, if the weather be fair and the fish amiable—there are few superior to that afforded by Tal-y-llyn.

At the mouth of Llyn Mwyngyl lies Tal-y-llyn, consisting of half-a-dozen straggling grey houses, a tiny church copse-hidden, a bridge with two quaintly irregular arches, and the most comfortable lake-side inn in all Wales, decorated by the most charming of hostesses, one Mrs. Evans, whose courtesies—photographical, prandial, and social—are largely and gratefully related in our travellers' note-books.

Tal-y-llyn is essentially a fishing station. Year after year the same well-known lake-*habitués* recur, each with his large portmanteau-like fly-book of London-made Tal-y-llyn-flies, his ancient and trustworthy lake-rod, his trout-basket weather-stained, fish bearing. Year after year the same fish-killing process recurs also. There are four or five large and clumsily-built sea-boats belonging to the inn: each boat is manned by two fishermen, who row to the windward shore of the lake, lower a large stone attached by a long rope to the thwarts amidships, and float slowly down to leeward, catching fish or not as they go. On the lee shore the stone is shipped, and the process is repeated *ad infinitum*. From 7 to 9 a.m., from 10 to 4 p.m., from 5 to 9, the lake is dotted with these wandering craft, and the number of fish consequently slain is, per annum, certainly great. Four dozen trout (averaging three to a pound) per rod, per diem, have been, and may be, killed by experienced Tal-y-lynn fishermen in favourable weather; the visitors' book, however, recounts more failures than successes. The lake, nevertheless, is one of the best trout-lakes, if not *the* best lake, in Wales; the practice of netting it is at last discontinued, and a good fisherman, with a light cast of flies, will doubtlessly have good sport therein in good weather, more than which cannot be said of any trout-water, whether lake or stream.

Jonas White inspected the lake before breakfast, on the first morning after his arrival, in his own fashion. Crossing the bridge, he walked by the shore under the base of Cader Idris, till he came to the alluvial flats and the marshes at the head of the lake, through and over which he floundered and leaped—resembling, as Abraham said, who was watching him telescopically from an advantageous eminence—a strong-minded and able-bodied crane, who did not find remunerative feeding in his present diggings, and was determined to seek fresh fields and pastures new, with the smallest possible loss of time. Then he returned by the Tal-y-llyn shore, and climbed up to the summit of the torrent-seamed hills above the village, in order to get a general and hawk's-eye view of the neighbourhood: finally he came down a torrent-bed after the manner of a frost-loosened boulder, and returning to breakfast, announced that he had been out for a stroll and was rather hungry.

Abraham. "I should like to know whether, after all my panegyrics, you are disappointed with Llyn Mwyngyl and its neighbourhood, because I fancy it is a place which grows on a man, and I could imagine that it might not be sufficiently wild and 'mountaneous' for you on first impressions."

Jonas (in the intervals of high breakfast). "Not a bit. It has two charms which are more than charming to me. It's very complete, and it's very suggestive."

Abraham. "Well: go on."

Jonas. "Why you see *quâ* lake it's a model lake: shape good; a delicate and graceful oval: proportion good, as three to one; it's not narrow enough to be a *fac simile* of a sluggish river, not broad enough to be a fat, squabby, hill-side pool: colour good; not so shallow as to be a mere sky-mirror, not so deep as to be black, cold, dreary, but with a bright, clear, sparkling sunny blue of its own. Then it's suggestive: northward is that shelving gorge reaching from the marshes to white Trigaianen high among the hills; eastward are these stream-torn precipices, telling many a story of stormy winter nights, when the voices of the torrents are lifted up on the high mountains, when the winds scream and wail like lost spirits in desolate places, when the rain welters on the bleak hill-sides, and the boulder-stones roar and crash together for joy of the power that is come among them, as the white-foamed waters sweep them down in endless avalanche-falls to their resting places in the reeking cloud-veiled valleys below; then southward there is the quiet valley where the black Bird-rock stands, a solitary watch-tower between the purple hill-country and the fragrant sea; westward lies the height, and depth, and fullness of the great Cader—there it lies, as my soul knoweth well, though I can but see the sullen sweep of its mighty base, ravine-cleft, stream-jewelled, wood-wreathed, mirrored deeply in the blue Mwyngyl; above, beyond, what wealth of unsullied nature is there not? What hidden precipices scarped and battered by all the storms of God—what fathomless tarns, now grim and voiceless, in bygone ages craters of living, hurtling fire—what waste places, grey-rock-strewn, of dry and rustling grass, vocal with all sweet mountain music, when the strong north wind sweeps along in his cloud-compelling resonant might —what solitary peaks above the rolling vapours, star-lit, serene, beautiful! Some more tea, if you please."

Abraham. "Incorrigible! I sometimes think that your final bathos is introduced for the sake of contrast, just as one sketches in a figure beneath a lofty tower, to give the building its relative and true size."

Jonas. "No, indeed. I asked for the tea because I was thirsty. Don't ever think that

I talk for talking's sake, or I shall be mute to you for evermore—no great loss to you by the way. As I think, so I speak, and great mountains make one think if one's soul be ever capable of that exercise. And now for our rods, and all the trout in Tal-y-llyn before nightfall."

Abraham. "Yes: for at Tal-y-llyn there is a common

> 'lot for all,
> That each from what they dearest call,'

whether botanizing, photographising, or mountain-climbing,

> 'Shall sever,'

and shall sit from early morn till dewy eve in the tubbiest and flat-bottomest of boats, flogging the patient waters 'for ever and for ever.' But let us go, for there is a hopeful ripple on the lake; and I, as an old Tal-y-llyn fisherman, have a *corps de reserve* in my fly-book, which, failing coch-y-bonddus, will do us good service."

So they embarked and were soon floating up the lake before the southerly wind. The fish rose freely, but rose "short," turning the fly over, breaking the water before it came to them, or leaping over it—"a sign of bad sport to come" said Abraham—who worked hard; and between them both there were quickly some three or four dozen yellow-sided captives in the bottom of the boat. Then there came a long pause—plenty of flogging, and no rises.

Abraham. "The fish don't seem to care about us. There is the best ground in the lake, in those shallows among the weeds. Now for my last resource. If they won't rise at coch-y-bonddus there is only one other thing at which they will rise: for Tal-y-llyn fish are like young ladies in a ball-room, when, if there be a sprinkling of red-coats, woe be to the black-coated gentry. Here is a page of scarlet in my fly-book; look, it doesn't matter, take one or any—a red hackle and a black body; a black hackle and a red body. Here is Shaw's invincible, here is my own inevitable."

Jonas (after a pause, during which the scarlet flies told well). "My theory of flies is a simple one, and I believe heterodox—but however!—When the fish rise freely one fly is as good as another, and better—for you lose time by changing. When there is a special fly on the water, as the coch-y-bonddu, use that; else, use dark flies on a bright day, and light-coloured flies on a dark day. When the fish don't rise freely, then tempt them with abnormalities, maggot flies, fancy flies, scarlet and gold flies: for I think that in well-fished lakes or streams, when the same flies have been passed over the same fish half-a-dozen times in the day, there must be a feeling of saminess in the proceedings to him, and like ourselves he must be inclined to prefer anything which is only more tempting because it is novel."

Abraham. "I agree with you on the whole: but I expect that an old-school fisherman would howl at your doctrine. He would have special flies for every locality, for every month of the year, and every time of the day. But I too am inclined to hold the ultra fly-book learning in some contempt, and I believe that your general principles with light tackle, and the lightest throwing, will fill a basket as surely and more rapidly than the practice of the ancient theorists."

Jonas. "And I'll tell you another thing worth knowing. On rough-weather days after a flood, or on bright days when the fish are not rising, one may do much with a cast of heavy flies, if one sinks them well in rapid water. At the tail of a 'run' one may kill fish in that way, when the orthodox surface fisherman is anathematizing the weather and his destiny in vain."

Abraham. "Ah, I know that plan well; for in some of the Devonshire rivers they run out thirty or forty yards of line, with a cast of a dozen flies at the end, under bridges, and down reaches overhung with feathering trees, and they pull out heavy fish, and plenty of them, which one could not reach in any other way. They sometimes use a fly with a twisted gutta-percha body and a black hackle, which, under water, kills well."

So conversing—"talking shop" if you will —and after all, men to succeed in the shop, must be of the shop, shoppy; and if the sugar is to be sanded one may as well get an additional opinion as to the quantity of sand required for a given quality of sugar in stock —so conversing, they fished on till the sun was high and fervent in mid-sky, and the lake a glittering sheet of liquid silver, and the trout were poised motionlessly in the green weed-thickets: and then with one consent they pulled up steadily to the windward shore of the lake, and there as the drifting-stone fell with a cool and sudden plash into the circling water, they laid rod and labour together aside, and drifted calmly down the calm-wind-stream, lapsing by insensible degrees into a silence taught of nature in the mid-reign of the golden summer and the fiery sun.

O happy summer days so spent in most prolific idleness! For by-and-bye as the light westered and a cooler breeze sprung up from the far-off sea, and the boat swung in mid-water under the central-climbing gorge of

Cader, what joyful resurrection of mountain-life sprang up in that distant solitude!

Far over head the white-winged gull sailed, noiselessly, as it were a flitting cloudlet in the deep-blue sky: on the mountain the raven belled* from his lonely crag: the large black cormorant, the trout-poacher, the ill-scented, skimmed along the surface of the lake with outstretched neck and cruciform sheeny wing: the water-hen dabbled busily in and out among the rushes and the delicate water-copses of pale-lilac lobelia: the corn-crake shrilled etèrnally in the waving meadow-grass: the wood-pigeon crooned soothingly in the shadowy mountain-thickets.

Now and then a wandering shape of whitest cloud threw a grey shadow over the burning hills: now and then the fickle wind whispered in the sedges and died away on the glittering

---

* A raven does *not* croak: there is a clear, musical ring in his cry which distinguishes him from all other corvi.

lake: now and then a heavy plash and a circle of dying ripples told that a lazy trout had bestirred himself, and was gone to his cool depths again.

Abraham. "Did I tell you, Jonas—I don't think I did—that Caroline will probably join us when we settle down somewhere or other about Snowdon,—perhaps at Pen-y-gwryd? You know Pen-y-gwryd?—a quiet moor-side inn, out of the way of the tourist tribe, whom I have the lack of charity to abhor on these occasions, and—"

Jonas. "Confound this pipe—it will *not* light."

And he hurled the fuzee far away into the lake, where it sputtered, and died out, and floated away reproachfully.

There was silence again for a while, during which Abraham's thoughts wandered far away from Caroline and Jonas and Tal-y-llyn; and Jonas resolved many things earnestly which stirred his strong man's heart to its very core.

At length as the evening shadows were stealing up the quiet mountain, and the stranded boat was swaying idly in the marish sedges, and the sun was sinking in the long valley—an orb of gold in emerald mist, Jonas roused himself with a quick effort, and with set lips and a strange worn look about his eyes said,

"After all, I fancy my stay in Wales will not be so long a one as I had anticipated."

Abraham. "My dear Jonas, what on earth do you mean by that very unpleasant observation *apropos* of nothing at all?"

Jonas. "Why I am sorry to say that 'circumstances over which I have no control' have lately arisen which necessarily shorten my mountain rambling—and I have been trying to see how my plans can be made to dovetail into yours. You said some short time ago that your sister means to join you; I conclude you will take a temporary run out of Wales for the purpose of escorting her; and if so, it might be at a time when it would suit me to go a part of the way with you on my permanent and undesirable return."

Abraham (mentally, in a pause of apparent

consideration). "My dull eyes are beginning to open at last. Either I must be a very indifferent whip, or my team must be an uncommonly bad one to manage. First of all the wheeler shies, kicks, and finally runs away; and then, just as I am getting her in hand again, the leader takes the bit in his mouth and prepares to bolt round 'all manner of corners.' But the tackle won't hold if I pull him up too suddenly." (Aloud.)—"You don't generally take unnecessary freaks into your head, Jonas, and so I must suppose that there is some urgent reason for this unexpected change of plan. However I should be very sorry that my sister should lose the pleasure of rambling about Snowdon with us both; so what say you to steering for Pen-y-gwryd at once, (fishing here is evidently useless till the rain comes,) and then I would fetch her without loss of time, and we might have a week or so together before you are obliged to leave."

This was bringing matters to a crisis. Jonas saw no obvious means of escape, and he hated concealment of all kinds, and on principle met a difficulty promptly and boldly. So he sat upright in the boat, and with a pale but determined face began again.

"I am not fond of talking about myself, but there are times when such a proceeding is necessary, and I see it must be so now. You know my circumstances as well as I know them myself—how that by no fault of mine I have come down from riches to poverty, and can hardly by hard labour gain for my mother and sister the ordinary comforts of life which are necessary for them. So that (having no prospects whatever of rising, so long as I remain with them) it would be utterly absurd and wicked in me to think of taking to myself a wife.

"Now—and here is my confession, which for my sins I see I have to make—my own impracticable day-dream of life is connected with your sister. I have fought hard against it; but there are things against which no man can fight successfully unless he be prepared to throw overboard all individuality and natural feeling; this is one of those matters, and there it is, and there it will remain—my one hopeful blessing in life although my one hopeless hope.

"Ten years ago, heir to some few thousands a-year, I might have cherished a trust that, in time, my hopes would have been realized; now, it would be worse than folly to foster that which, if realized, would socially lower her for whom I care—would bring her, at all events, in some connection with that poverty which individually I can bear well enough. You know that I have never spoken to her on the subject, and I think you know that I never will; and, therefore, you must see that I must not cross her path again. Of course, the meeting would be indifferent to her; but, to me, she can never be as an ordinary woman—and so

'The mighty wind ariseth roaring seawards—
and I go.'

Now, please don't give me any answer, for the present, at all events. Despise my weakness and folly if you will; but respect my resolution.

"So let it be."

Abraham knew his friend well, and knew men well: at all events, he had studied them long and manfully, and valued the knowledge of that kind which he had acquired more than any other knowing of his.

A weak man would have desired in his inner soul to have been encouraged; would plan a sacrifice, and, perhaps, carry it out, if he were not solicited, worried, forced, as he would say, not to sacrifice himself. Then he sacrifices another person, and, on the whole, is better pleased with the result.

A man of will, determined to carry out what he has willed, such a man meets with difficulties so habitually, that, at last, difficulties are necessary to his comfort; he looks out for opposition, meets it when he can, makes it when he cannot meet it. If such a man is to be guided in a direction contrary to his present will, it is useless to oppose barriers to his course. Let us go with that man, and, by-and-bye, suggest the difficulties which lie on the return route.

Abraham looked his friend fully and anxiously in the eyes, and having filled his pipe during the process, only answered,

"Give me a light, will you?"

Then they shoved the boat into deep water, and pulled steadily up the lake in the track of the sinking sun—steadily with an even stroke—Jonas pulling stroke.

Up from the sea came the fresh night wind. The scarlet clouds, high in the west, watching the great sun Atlantic-borne through endless day, faded into crimson, into violet, into greyblue, into murky grey; star by star the night crept on; through the woods on the left flank of Cader the moon looked, making a blaze of full soft light in the falling of a white stream, before unseen—and their boat grated sharply on the strand at Tal-y-llyn.

Abraham fastened the painter to a rusty iron-ring on the piles of the landing-place, now glittering black against the glittering moonlight; and then with one accord, as they stood on the shore together, with one accord, as if common nature and common friendship would have it so, they looked each other full in the face, and joined hands; and, with that full grasp in their hearts, walked into the small inn-room, and sat down contentedly to a late supper, and the other creature comforts necessary to sentient and rational beings.

Those ancient *habitués* of Tal-y-llyn certainly "rule the roast," the split fried trout (no other cooking of trout so good), the nightly whisky-and-water, and the other arrangements of the inn, with an autocratic hand.

Republics of temperate-minded men, are, when autocratic, successful institutions.

The Tal-y-llyn fishermen-republic is most autocratic: at such an hour is general breakfast, at such an hour general dinner (late comers breakfast and dine on remains), during such hours we fish, during such hours we converse of fish. There is a president of the republic, who wears the inn-slippers, and sits in the inn-easy-chair, and is garnished with flies in a dangerous but convenient manner; he promulgates the laws of the state, and does the inn manners to the new comers, and puts the inn-candles out at midnight.

There is the inn-republic orator, a shiny-headed, beetle-browed man, with thick-edged garments, and a pervading sense of tackle to be arranged for to-morrow about him. He harangues the republic interminably, and kotoos the president (with a very large P), and is affable to the juniors, and fills up all pauses with fish-tattle and fishing legends which have no beginning or end, and he will not be so successful to-morrow as one might expect him to be.

But republics, like some other institutions, sleep at times; and so when the forty-ninth story of the orator had satisfactorily arrived at what was probably its middle, the president put out the candles, and the institution retired to its bed; save and except Abraham and Jonas, who surreptitiously returned from dark corners in the passage, relighted the presidentially-extinguished candles, and composed themselves for another quiet pipe, and a little friendly chat.

"I abhor a man," said Jonas, with a savage jerk, "who has got his mouth full of stories on a subject."

Abraham. "Well, I don't altogether disapprove of him; he fills up the gaps of silence, and gives one an opportunity of not listening to him."

Jonas. "O, he may be useful in that way; but a man cannot tell a story unless he has the dramatic element in his composition—and nine men in ten have not; moreover, he must be epigrammatically-minded to turn his points neatly; and discriminatively-minded to select his epithets tellingly; and humanly-minded to give us pathos; and grotesquely-minded to give us the sunshine of pure humour. That bald bullet-headed man who has gone, at last, to his rest, is a mass of mere facts, which he pours out in a leaden stream, so many per minute, like a well-oiled Colt's-revolver."

Abraham. "Mere fact, is, I think, somewhat pernicious. When a boy I remember undergoing a course of 'Percy Anecdotes' in some fifteen or twenty volumes duodecimo. I arose from the perusal of that fearful work without a single fresh idea, or (for which I am truly grateful) without having a single anecdote impressed on my memory."

Jonas. "Yes, that is an example in point. A story which is dramatic, imaginative, grotesque, human, lives in one's mind, and is 'a joy for ever;' a mere anecdote, the relation of a bare event which appeals to nothing divine or human in one's heart, is like a pebble thrown into that lake, it disturbs the calm for an instant, and sinks, happily, into obscurity and oblivion."

Abraham. "I think that your 'story' is to your 'anecdote,' what a friend is to an acquaintance."

Jonas. "Eh?"

Abraham. "A friend appeals to the imaginative, humorous, human element, and remains 'a joy for ever;' an acquaintance is but one's relation to some chance event, is merely circumstantial, and dies out with the death of the circumstances."

Jonas. " Good. When I was at Oxford, the only work (work necessary, I mean) which ever fairly interested me was 'Aristotle.' I don't think I ever arrived at construing him in a scholarly manner, but I got to make out his meaning more or less, and he used to set me thinking, which was always a pleasure; and I recollect being considerably given to musing on the VIIIth and IXth Books—about friendship."

Abraham. " Did he generally agree with you ?"

Jonas. " In some respects more or less. But I remember arranging in a sequence the different states of feeling which he describes under the head of friendship, and working out a theory of progress which satisfied me. I have almost forgotten my 'Aristotle' in my pursuit of pounds, shillings, and pence, but this was the theory as I recollect it; more of mine, perhaps, than his."

Abraham fills another pipe, and composes himself.

Jonas. "I began with a state of things which was in fact a practical agreement existing between two people in matters of life and politics, (not that I took much interest then in politics, but Aristotle's 'politics' were not coincident with those of our time;) a state it was which cared less for the persons who agreed than for their agreement. Similarity of purpose, and recognition of humanity in varying shapes therewith conjoined.

"Then followed, between the two given persons, the instinct we have of loving men for their good qualities; our natural cleaving to a man who is a man and means well.

"Then came a mutual readiness to do good to and oblige and help a man of that sort.

"This state of feeling might branch in two directions.

"If it benefited an inferior in station and intellect, thence ensued the contemplative benevolence which is the result of a benefaction—the benefactor's view of his *protégé*.

"But if it benefited an equal—you see it *must* benefit somebody—it went on to friendliness, a state of feeling and action which, when it became reciprocal and habitual, ripened into true 'friendship'—friendship being a settled state of active good-will existing between two persons who are aware of each other's preference and intentions."

Abraham (who has not had time to doze). "Well then, leaving Aristotle (which I am not much acquainted with), you think that similarity is the basis of friendship, do you? And yet you and I differ as much as any two men could do; you are energetic, enthusiastic: I am cool, calm, calculating."

Jonas. "My dear Abraham, you must have been snoring during my ethical lecture. Similarity, no! a thousand times: but similarity of purpose, yes! You and I have the same great theories of life, though you may be a Conservative, and I a Liberal. We care for the same greatness and goodness in all great and good men, and in all great and good books. In details we may and must differ, but in principle we are the same; just as two oaks are oaks alike, though no two branches or leaves of them are alike."

Abraham. "Don't you think that *dis*-similarity of *character* is a fair basis of friendship?"

Jonas. "But how?"

Abraham. "I grant all your position about the necessity of a prior similarity of life-aims; a coincidence of Platonic ideas, —mental patterns of things that should be, and are not. When that state of things exists in the case of two individuals, they may be firm friends if circumstance so allow it; but I think that they are more likely to be attracted to each other if they are in temperament somewhat dissimilar. The cool, calm, calculating man, who in his heart honours enthusiasm and energy, is drawn to a friend in whose character those features are prominent. The energetic man has suffered for want of calmness, and admires the man who is cool and calculating. One friend fills up the void places, and satisfies the cravings of the other friend.

"Together there results a self-compensating balance which tends to a perfect machine."

Jonas. "Yes, yes; and the motive power is one and the same—similarity of life-ends. The machine on the whole is a very perfect one, though it may rust sometimes for want of use."

Abraham. "And there is one more thing which I must add before I go to bed, although my pipe is out, and I hugeously sleepy. You philosophers do not in general give sufficient scope to the friend who is not in need when he would help the friend who therein is. You say (at least Aristotle does —almost the only thing I remember of him), —that a needy or unfortunate man should go reluctantly to a friend if it be to share with him his good fortune. That may be true for the needy friend in one respect, but I think that it is selfish of him. He may consult his own independence, his own self-denial, and what not, by so refraining; but he does not consult his friend's well-being. Throughout your lecture, which I liked, you said that friendship was benefit; a man must *quâ* friend do good to his friend. The needy man, therefore, should go willingly to his friend who has all and abounds, and be glad that he can be a subject on which can be exercised the highest offices, the very essence, of his friend's friendship. It is pride, selfishness, weakness, which would make a man eat a crust uncomplainingly in a garret, when his friend (mind his friend in the highest, only true sense of the word) is dining on turtle and venison in a gorgeously decorated saloon. The crust so eaten is sweet enough, I know well, but a truer friend would go down to his friend in the lower room.

"And now to bed—and we'll get up early and photograph the great crater of Llyn Cac, before to-morrow's sun leaves its western precipices."

Jonas followed meditatively, and by-and-bye threw his boots down on the passage-floor outside his bed-room door as though they had been something heavy on his mind of which he was desirous to rid himself.

CHAPTER IV.

THE GIANT'S THRONE.

AFTER the earliest possible breakfast the expedition started for the mountain lake in the following order:—First and foremost was Jonas White, who totally eschewed guides and guidance on principle, and usually lost himself and his ordnance map with much success. His camera was slung across his shoulder, and the "legs" neatly strapped together were to do duty as alpen-stock, if such a thing should be necessary. Then followed the guide, a tall, raw-boned, thin-visaged, red-nosed, red-haired native who had evidently imbibed too much "Cwrw" on the previous night, and was now paying the penalty of his excesses by suffering from impaired digestion and temper; he owned to feeling "ferry pât inteet," and carried a private soda-water bottle of raw whisky—as medicine. He bore the photographic apparatus of Abraham, who followed calmly smoking his pipe, and trailing a long ashen iron-shod mountain-pole which he had borrowed from Mrs. Evans, with his usual foresight.

It was one of those windless amber-tinted mornings which in the mountains are the sure prognosticators of a day of burning heat. There was a yellow shimmering mist hanging in the gorge northward of the lake, and one or two masses of round white cloud were travelling very slowly along the hill-crests in the East. The Tal-y-llyn fishermen were already at work, but the fish were not rising, and did not mean to rise till the white clouds had gathered into thunder peaks, and the lashing rain had filled the dry torrent-beds once more with life and music.

The expedition crossed the bridge and followed the right bank of the lake till they came to the central ravine of which we have before spoken—and then the ascent began.

For awhile a scarcely-marked sheep-track led them along a shelving ledge of loose shale and rolling stones, through low thickets of furze and fern, and past sheltered nooks of crag and boulder, where the mountain flowers had made unregarded gardens for themselves wherein they might rejoice in their own delicacy and fragrance. There were the curved coronets of the sun-dew (*Drosera rotundifolia*); each red and green leaf set thickly with glittering points of light; the pale yellow rosettes of *Pinguicula*; the golden petals of the small S. John's-wort (*Hypericum pulchrum*), the scented fronds of *Lastrea Oreopteris*; the upright red rough stems and glossy green leaflets of the Male Fern (*Lastrea Filix-mas, var. Borreri:*) these and many more made the mountain base populous with beauty of form and colour, as all such solitudes are to those whose eyes are not closed by carelessness and ignorance.

The sheep-track ceased suddenly, and then

they emerged on a grassy slope which commanded a view of the whole lake and its terminal valleys.

The day was scorching, the short grass and the sphagnum beds were painfully hot to the touch, the lurid mist had risen, and not a cloud dimmed the glare of the burning sun, nor a breath of air cooled the fiery landscape.

But still the path lay onward and upward, and in life it does not answer to turn back, even on an excursion of pleasure.

So onward and upward panted the expedition, clearing presently the line of ordinary vegetation, and entering the region of mountain grass. Onward still, along a ledge of slippery shale, barely wide enough for the feet, below which lay a wild waste of torn rock, painfully suggestive of broken bones, to a man whose head did not happen to be of the steadiest.

Then, again, an upward clamber on dry shining grass, specked with outcropping peaks of slate-rock, and gemmed with tufts of various club-mosses, now the erect plumes of *L.*

selago, now the creeping net-work of *clavatum*, now the lance-like leaflets of *alpinum*.

Jonas (perfectly breathless). "Abraham, would you have any objection to admire the prospect for a few minutes? My respect for Cader is painfully increasing."

Abraham (seating himself with much alacrity). "Yes; this is mountain pure and simple. Now Snowdon is degenerated into a pleasant promenade between an early breakfast and a late lunch: in fact they have so be-pathed that ill-used mountain, and so surrounded him with fashionable hotels, and ascended him with scientific guides, and crowned him with houses and bitter-beer-bottles, that he always reminds me of a lion in a travelling menagerie, caged, cramped, voiceless, spiritless, the inevitable result of a civilization which pampers curiosity and eschews knowledge."

Jonas. "The Americans, though, lick creation in that respect: they can breed a man to turn summersaults on a tight-rope which hangs thread-like above the eternal plunge of great Niagara; and, more hopeless still, they can produce an audience of 15,000 citizens, who exult in the feat, and are nationally proud of the performer."

Abraham. "*Apropos* of which I may mention, that a Devonshire farmer once adduced to me, as an instance of the evils of over-education, the case of a servant-girl of his, who exercised her powers of writing by scribbling in large chalk-letters on all his farm-gates, 'No thorough-fare,' her mathematical genius by doing sums (in chalk) on his front door, and her capabilities of reading by mastering the contents of every letter and bill of his on which she could lay her hands. Here (he said in effect), here's the mischief of all your parish schools. If the girl had never been taught to read, write, and cypher, she would not have damaged my property, and would have made me a good servant."

Jonas. "*Apropos?* Eh? Which?"

Abraham. "Why, I mean that as under-teaching ruined the servant, not over-teaching, as the farmer believed, so, similarly, under not over-civilization crowns Snowdon with twin rival 'hotels,' and produces a crowd of rational beings in all lands, who love to desecrate Nature with unnatural frivolity, and unreasoning childishnesses."

Jonas. "Yes, I see, of course; and so one may hope, even in such apparently hopeless circumstances, for 'the thoughts of men' *must* 'widen in the process of the suns,' and one day the caged lion of knowledge shall be set free, and the desert-ranger led by his mistress-queen, Una, the all-pure, the all-beautiful, shall roam through the world and be honoured by the many, as he is now neglected and scorned by them."

Abraham. "Utopian! And yet I have hope for civilization; seeing that the typical 'gentleman' is held daily in more esteem, and is daily multiplied in all classes of society."

Jonas. "What is a gentleman?"

Abraham. "One, who neither in thought, word, nor deed, hurts the feelings of those with whom he has to do."

Jonas. "A good definition. And of education?"

Abraham. "I have hopes of that too: for men are ceasing to confound it with instruction. Our schools will gradually give up the practice of merely cramming labourers' sons and daughters with dead facts of history, geography, and what not; will teach children to obey, to think, to reason, to take a human interest in learnt facts. Then, having educated, one can hardly over-instruct.

"And, moreover, the cuckoo-cry against education must die out; the cry, I mean, which is founded on the objection that education, beyond a certain point, tends to throw a man out of his station in life. For as is the demand for labourers, house-servants, and what not, so must be the supply; there will always be a per centage of individuals who will be able to get their living more easily in that way than in other ways—of such, they who have learnt best to know, to think, to obey, will be the best servants.

"If from station, opportunity, and so on,

I found a farm-bailiff's life that in which I could best earn a living which I must earn, I should not make a worse bailiff than the man I now employ, though I know somewhat of chemistry, natural history, and languages, of which he is deeply ignorant."

Jonas. "Just as our guide would be all the more efficient if he could tell us something about the mountain flora and fauna, and were aware that that bottle of his contained more alcohol than is good for his mucous membranes.

"But let us start again for our last pull: I know we must be near the high country by the sound."

Abraham. "The sound—what sound?"

Jonas. "Why that wonderful sound which the wind makes in high mountain places—always makes in such places, even when no wind can be felt to blow—sighing in the dry stiff grass-beds: wandering fitfully in and out of the many-angled crags: sweeping up the steep rock-scarps: swooping down into the still mountain curves, where the lakes ripple and glitter in the blazing sunlight.

"A sound which, I know full well, sunk deep into the inmost soul of him who first thought out the poetry that was in him in those grand old Organ fugues, which will live so long as music lives in the hearts of men. Do you not know how one hears, first of all, the few plain simple notes which give the subject—just the ripple of the mountain-wind in the grass at one's feet: how then it is taken up, now here, now there; doubling, redoubling, wandering, repeating; whispering among the high clear reeds, booming from the great metal diapasons, piping on the soft flute of the choir; now rising and falling on the swell, now bursting out in endless volume on the full great-organ. Never the same, and always the same, for ever in it all comes back the few plain simple notes of the burthen—just as the mountain echoes are now dying away, and the unfelt wind is rustling again monotonously in the dry stiff grass at our feet.

"But let us come onwards—one may think and talk for ever in these mountain solitudes, Heaven's own earthly temples of reverent thought and free-born knowledge—let us come on: the day is growing older and harder featured, and the lake is above us, and our dinner (to which consummation we must come at last) is far below us in that valley of cloud and sunlight."

Another ten-minutes' climb brought them to the summit of the left ridge of the higher lake-valley, and after a short and rapid descent, they stood by the verge of the still dark water.

Abraham. "If I wanted to describe this remarkable tarn with the greatest possible amount of clearness, I think I should endeavour to describe it historically."

Jonas. " Hypothetical history?"

Abraham. " Well, yes, of course; but probable history—as all geological history should be—history which accounts for a given formation, and is so far true, as the formation is thereby accounted for more reasonably than by any other theory."

Jonas (who is putting his rod together, and has his mouth full of flies). " Proceed."

Abraham. "Ages ago,—who shall say how many ages ago?—this rent and scarped mountain was, as I suppose, a vast and even mound, rounded and smoothed it may be by the action of the same mighty glacial drift whose footprints are still so legible in this land of hills. Underneath the thin and deceptive crust of primal rock surged and boiled fathomless volcanic cauldrons, which in the slow action of former ages had slowly upheaved the masses both of Cader and of Snowdon. At last the pent-up fires escaped, no longer repressible, into the light of day. Three or four craters opened out with a mighty burst around the central peak, and the mountain was torn, and twisted, and shattered with the great convulsion, and the whole country-side deluged with the up-heaved and widely-scattered rock. Here is the main crater of that period, perfectly conical in form, tapering from the summit of those opposite precipices to the very bottom of the lake—hitherto unfathomed—see there is deep water two feet off the shore. Then one side, the lowest and thinnest, of the crater, gave way, and the fire-stream opened out and rushed down the mountain over the spot where we stand."

Jonas. "'*Hinc illæ lacrymæ.*' That is to say, so you account for this chaos of big acute-angled rocks over which I have broken one, if not both, of my shins."

Abraham. "And then in due time when the fires had sunk to their former level, and the mountain became silent and grass-grown, the hill-springs gravitated into these dead furnace-holes, and the crater became a lake— as fiery youth lapses into kindly and beneficent age."

Jonas. "Ah! I see! Fire *versus* ice theories. And now, while you prove the truth of your opinions by picking up volcanic specimens on the lake-side, I shall go and see if I can't pick up a trout or two out of your furnace-hole. Perhaps if I allure the grandfather of all fishes out of these primæval depths, he will know as much about the matter as we do."

Jonas, however, fished with more perseverance than success. Llyn Cae trout are by no means to be caught napping. The lake is surrounded by deep precipices on three sides, and therefore is affected only by a steady wind from the North or the East. On the present occasion the wind was a light one from the South-west, and Jonas fished, and Abraham fished very much in vain. But their guide was wiser than they; he wandered round to the lee side of the lake, and with a long and clumsy rod threw a light line in the wind's eye whenever a slight ripple flew across the water, and by-and-bye he had a fair show of fish in his basket, and plainly viewed with contempt the unsuccessful tactics of the strangers.

Then the cameras were put into action; and then there was a meditative pipe or two under the shade of a big boulder; and so home, returning by another and easier route which descends a steep and brushwood-clad ravine at the end of Llyn Mwyngyl.

Here they came upon the promised marshes,

and though the daylight was beginning to wane, and a cool sea-breeze to ruffle the grey and gold waters of the lake, there was a pause made and an active search instituted for the benefit of the herbarium.

The search was by no means unprolific, and space would fail us in these sketches were we to attempt a flora of this or any given district in the land of mountains.

Jonas (decorating his wide-awake with sprigs of Bog-myrtle from the low glistening thickets, which richly scented the evening air). "I should like to filch the name of 'Traveller's Joy' from our English clematis, and transfer it to this useful plant."

Abraham. "And wherefore?"

Jonas. "Why don't you remember Mr. Metcalfe's hint in that pleasant book of his, 'The Oxonian in Thelemarken?' He says that the peasants make a decoction of the Bog-myrtle and sprinkle it about their houses because the fleas have a mortal horror of the proceeding. And he adds that he used to sleep with a branch or two of it under his pillow, and in his bed whenever he got into suspicious quarters, and that he always slept the more soundly in consequence. I have tried the plan myself, and not, I think, without benefit."

Abraham. "Ah! that is worth knowing, for one does not love the British kangaroo, and he is no rarity even in a tourist's fashionable hotel. But only look at the countless spires of yellow asphodel with their sheaves of pointed sword-leaves; and the white flags of the cotton-grass, and the broad foliage of the Bog-bean! and—ah! there in the midst of that squadron of orchises is *O. latifolia,* which one can't mistake because the bracts are longer than the flowers.

"Now come along, for our long-faced guide is getting horribly impatient—his whisky-bottle is finished ages ago, and Mrs. Evans is lighting her candles at Tal-y-llyn; see how the faint reflection is twinkling on the Lake. And there is the first star rising above the purple hill-line. Come, for the night comes, and the dew falls, and I hear the white owls hooting in the mountain-thickets—and man, being mortal, must have his supper, though science were to perish from the earth in the interval."

Note inserted for the benefit of the travelling photographer. Beware of the Llyn Mwyngyl water. It is perfectly " soft;" *but* it is charged with iron, and probably other metals, and will infallibly ruin the developer. The natives seldom save rain-water, as the lake-water answers for all domestic purposes.

CHAPTER V.

FROM CADER TO SNOWDON.

THE next day was devoted to photography, and not altogether in vain.

On the following morning at a very early hour Jonas was pervading the neighbouring granary and the house generally, in a high state of activity—now presenting himself at unexpected corners laden with cargoes of bottles and fragile glass-ware—now descending the stairs heavily with a heavy portmanteau on his back—now knocking cheerily at Abraham's door with reiterated shouts, loud enough to waken the Seven Sleepers, of "Inspann and Trek! Trek and Inspann!" Presently at the inn-door appeared Abraham's face, fresh and calm, and beaming with good temper, against whom tumbled Jonas in a state of vast excitement, and at a very abnormal temperature, bearing a vast freight of coats and wrappers wherewith to fill up the interstices of the packed-up packing-case.

"Well," he said, "it's all done, Abraham. While you were snoring "Judy" was decently interred in her mausoleum. Whatever have you been sleeping in such an aggravated manner for? Why it's any hour of the clock!"

Abraham. "I don't see how any one could sleep while you go up and down the house like a waterspout, shrieking out in unknown tongues at middle-aged gentlemen's bed-room doors. What in the name of goodness is that barbaric formula with which you have apparently been endeavouring to exorcise me, or the spirit of sleep in me, for the last hour and a half?"

Jonas. "O, 'Trek and Inspann, Inspann and Trek!' Why, it's the signal-call of the Caffre-land Boors when they are making off for new diggings;

'In with your clothes
And off you goes!'

free translation ; Jonas White.

"But come along; swallow your breakfast; strap up your carpet-bags; pay your bill; and take a last look at the lake on the sunniest summer morning that ever was. We ought to be half-way to Dolgelley by this time."

And accordingly, urged by Jonas, whose spirits were at boiling point, the departure was quickly made, and ("Judy" with the rest of the luggage having been previously despatched in a country cart) the travellers were soon jogging along the lake-side in a two-wheeled Welsh car—of which conveyance it can only be said that the tourist gets as much exercise for his money as he can expect, and possibly a good deal more.

It takes a long pull and a strong one to climb the ravine which leads northwards from Llyn Mwyngyl. Near its summit is a tiny pool (Llyn Mach, or the little lake, in the vernacular) which bears a lengthy and somewhat unpronounceable name in the Ordnance Map. It is there called Llyn Trigraianen, or the Lake of the Three Pebbles—the three pebbles being three large boulders by its side, which are said to have been extracted by the Giant Idris from his boots, and to have been hurled by him from the top of Cader to their present position, in a temporary fit of anger— and doubtless it was trying to the temper of the giant to have had such irregular angularities in his Balmorals. After passing this lake the road descends, crossing a wild moorland country with Cader Idris, massive and gloomy, on the extreme left, and in front a fantastically broken outline of wooded hills, under one of which lies Dolgelley.

Dolgelley* is by no means a remarkable

---

* Botanical note by Jonas White:
    Dolgelley—Impatiens noli-me-tangere,
        Geranium lucidum,
        Epilobium roseum,
        Rumex sanguineus,
        Polypodium phegopteris.

place save to the traveller who will take the trouble of penetrating its byeways. On the banks of the rapid stream, whose bed is a very chaos of boulders and lime-stone rocks

> "Confusedly hurled,
> The fragments of a former world,"

are strung a series of boulder-built many-angled hovels and cottages, slate-roofed, lichen-covered, grey and cold, hanging over the stream, from whence their walls arose, picturesquely enough to gladden the eyes of the most fastidious of artists.

At Dolgelley there were letters—amongst others a letter from Caroline to Abraham :—

"Dearest Abey," so it began, "This is the most charming place in the world, and I don't know how I can ever leave it for Wales and you. Fancy a *very* old ivy-covered grange with gable ends, and twisted chimneys, and great buttresses, and deep porches, and projecting windows—such stone carving outside and such old oak carving inside—fancy this standing on the sunny side of a hill surrounded by great sweeping chestnuts and feathering limes : and then there are such great wandering gardens full of flowers and fruit, and such a park where the deer lie out in the tall fern coppices, and such a beautiful trout-stream, or almost river, in the middle of the park-valley.

"How you *would* enjoy yourself here, Mr. Abey—and like the Lees too I am sure. Mr. Lee, a jolly, deep-voiced, white-headed old Squire, riding about his grounds on his grey cob with half a score of greyhounds after him —Mrs. Lee, a fair, tall, stately gentlewoman, (that's the right word isn't it, Abey?) kind and unselfish and caring only that every one about her should be happy and comfortable. And as for Amy Lee, why, you know she's my best friend, and so she must be perfection, sir! But I must tell you what she is like if it is only to fill up my letter with the proper number of crossed lines. She is tall, a head and more taller than I am, with such a pliant and taper figure that it's quite a pleasure to watch her when she walks or runs—for we run wild about the park just as the deer do—she's got long black shining hair, and *such* eyes! And then she is so full of fun and merriness that it's like living with a sunbeam to be in the same house with her.

"She is just the active, good-tempered, cheery girl you would be sure to like—you dear sedate old Abey! And I've nearly persuaded her to come to Wales with me, but we think it wouldn't be *proper*—there now, don't get into a rage—to get into such wild places and bad company without a chaperone, and we can't entrap any old duenna who would be sufficiently locomotive and regardless of crinoline and best bonnets to suit us.

"But we shall see. At all events I want to know where you are going to settle down, and when you are coming to fetch me, and what you and Mr. White have been doing with yourselves—fishing and chemicalizing and smoking and conducting yourselves in a generally ne'er-do-well manner of course. So write soon,—and a long letter—and don't get Mr. White to direct it for you; for the last epistle of yours so endorsed wandered through all the country post-offices at hap-hazard, and finally came here as it went to other places just out of curiosity to see whether a 'Miss'—name illegible, dwelling at unreadable 'Grange,' post-town 'not known' anywhere, 'Staffordshire,' happened to be hereabouts residing.

" Always your affectionate Sister,

" C. B."

"Ah," said Abraham, when he had finished reading this letter aloud for the special benefit of Jonas, who pretended not to be listening with any perceptible amount of interest, and smiled grimly at the final allusion to his handwriting, " there is my luck again! To have a pair of untrained hawks on one's hands in a mountain country is a remarkably cheerful prospect! But we must arrange our plans for the next week nevertheless. Suppose then, Jonas, we make play for our abiding place under Snowdon—this Pen-y-gwryd about which I have told you, at the head of Llanberis Pass, and out of the run of 'tourists' whom my soul abhorreth! Suppose we arrive there, say in two days' time; and then I leave you whilst I go and bring back one, two, or three companions as the case may be; and afterwards we will have a comfortable three weeks' enjoyment of all sorts!"

Poor Jonas! To have all his stern resolutions and rigid sacrifices thrown to the winds by such an obvious speech, just as if no "confidences" had ever passed between Abraham and himself! He hesitated for an instant with a puzzled look, really not quite knowing whether Abraham had forgotten their evening's talk on Tal-y-llyn, and whether he would have to begin it all over again.

So Abraham taking advantage of the pause in a crafty manner went on, "You see, my dear Jonas, it's the only thing to be done. Caroline knows that all our plans have been settled even to the day of our return; and that you are to come back to Marscombe for a week before you go up to town: so that it's really too late to make any alteration now."

"BUT,"—began Jonas in a very loud voice, and with a very desperate expression of face —whereupon, Abraham beholding, had much ado to preserve a decorous gravity, and only after a great effort calmly interrupted his friend with,

"Now, Jonas, do be reasonable: get off those stilts (as if your own legs weren't long enough): take immense walks daily, and photograph, and fish, and botanize with all your might, *but at Pen-y-gwryd*. Depend upon it you will always be an unhappy man if you always fly from difficulties which you have previously made with a too successful ingenuity. There is no earthly reason why we should not all be jolly 'on the mountain.' You needn't quarrel with Caroline, and you needn't propose to her if you don't think it right so to do: and as you haven't done so, why you will meet her as you have always met—as friends and friends' friends. 'Che *sara sara.*' Don't worry yourself about unnecessary futures, and don't make us all unhappy on such a very lame plea."

During which oration, energetically delivered for Abraham, Jonas paced the coffee-room of "the Ship" like a caged lion, and ended by capsizing a waiter, tray and all, into the arms of an elderly gentleman in a white tie, which procession (consisting in fact of the gentleman and his dinner) had entered somewhat suddenly and certainly at an inauspicious instant. But the result of Abraham's lecture, and a long solitary walk which Jonas undertook at the conclusion of his apologies to the unfortunate and irate dinner-loser, was that Abraham was right and that he (Jonas) was a fool. "Double fool" he said to himself bitterly "to think that she or any girl in her circumstances would be likely to care a straw about a beggared banker's-clerk. Yes; Abraham is right. I will go; though I had rather ten thousand times over be counting the sparrows in Pump-alley from my long-legged stool than be tormented by——Hang it, what is it that Thackeray says—something about standing at the gate of Eden and watching an angel inside—said gate of course being barred, bolted, and locked with Chubb's double-acting thief-detectors. There—Jonas White is himself again! And after all there are worse things in the world than long-legged stools, angels, and patent-safety Chubbs."

After which somewhat incoherent soliloquy he faced about, and steadily marched innwards, announcing to Abraham on his arrival that his "urgent private affairs" should for the present be deferred, and that he had become after due consideration a convert to the arguments of his friend.

"Well," said Abraham, to himself, having duly expressed his pleasure at the change aloud, "so ends the first act. Act the second will bring all the characters on the stage, and I don't see my way to the catastrophe of the drama at all; for supposing that Caroline will have him, how they are to marry without prospects is much beyond my powers of understanding. But however—"

With which comprehensive conclusion he took up his bed-candle, and went to bed.

Our travellers took coach from Dolgelley to Beddgelert, a one-day's diorama of great variety and beauty. So up with the curtain and let the men at the winches turn as steadily as may be.

Here are the Rhine-lands of Wales; a broad winding tidal river wandering in and out between masses of waving wood and a rolling outline of margining hills. Those shining houses on the sandy shore down by the sea where the great herring-gulls are paddling and flapping about in the shoaling water? That is Barmouth.

And here comes a long, apparently endless stretch of alluvial lowlands, sown at intervals with white villages, and divided by rock-strewn torrent-beds. Westwards look at that shimmering reach of tawny sands, those low crumpled windy sandhills, and that great glittering sea with its far-off sail-flecked blue horizon-line. Eastward there are black and misty ravines, the moorland gates of the distant mountain country.

And here we have the king of Welsh castles, Harlech, throned on that peaked promontory which juts out into the plain. See how its grand and simple outlines stand out in radiant purple against the orange sands below!

Now we are skirting the shores of a wide estuary; here at its higher end is the pretty village of Maentwrog nestling against the side of a wood-covered hill; and here at its mouth again the great stone causeway of Port-madoc stretching sternly and strongly across the entrance of the Tremadoc vale, as though some huge giant's arm long since turned to stone were ever separating the fertile valley from the barren sea.

And now the woods grow denser and more frequent, and the hills are rising, and the streams narrowing and deepening, and so at last we draw near to the great Caernarvonshire mountain range.

Yes, here is Pont-Aberglasslyn, the greatest gateway of the great Welsh mountain land.

A scarped torrent-torn ravine—below a chaos of grey rock and rushing water, above an endless wave-line of rustling greenery. And still, beneath the fringes and festoons of that luxuriant vegetation lurk the scars of that tremendous old-world glacier-action, which reft and rounded and polished the slate and limestone formations of this wild district. And that is Beddgelert. O paint it for me, cunningest-handed of wandering artist folk; with silvery stream and gloaming wood in foreground of evening grey, and in the far-off cloudy distance the rolling surge of the everlasting hills, and Snowdon culminating all, alone among the shimmering summer stars!

That night under immense difficulties, in a saddle-room at a temperature of 90°, and with rain-water procured after an hour's conversation with a native "oat-stealer," who had one fixed idea that river-water was rain-water, and consequently must be what the "chentlemans" wanted, some more photographic work was accomplished; and the next morning Jonas and Abraham were on their road to their destination—now skirting the gloomy shores of Llyn Dinas, now lingering beside the wood-fringed lake of pleasant* Gwynnant. Then as they wound steadily round the bases of Snowdon the trees were left behind, and the mountains fern-covered boulder-sprinkled, rose grandly on all sides of them.

"There is Pen-y-gwryd at last," said Abraham, as the carriage crawled slowly to the very top of the pass.

And there it was, a solitary road-side inn, on a great table-land of windy mountain moors, at the head of three mountain passes.

"Northward," said Abraham, doing showman for Jonas' benefit, "are the grey crags of the desolate Glyders, southward the rounded grass-grown summit of Siabod, and westward

---

* Nant Gwynnant—Parnassia palustris,
Lobelia Dortmanni (in lake)
Achillæa Ptarmica.

(there!) the mighty mass of Snowdon—who from this side is a grand mountain in spite of cockneys and guide-books.

"And if we can't stay here for any length of time out of tourist range and within reach of some of the finest and most characteristic scenery that a lover of mountains can desire, I am sure that it will be our own fault, and not that of our landlord and guide-to-be, Henry Owen, whose good-tempered face is already gleaming a kindly welcome on us."

CHAPTER. VI.

HAWARDEN GRANGE.

WE will now leave Jonas White to explore Pen-y-gwryd and its neighbourhood for himself, and follow Abraham, who has already departed on his Staffordshire journey. And this arrangement is necessary for our story's sake.

His travels need not detain us.

There was an early, very early morning drive past the Capel Curig Lakes, cold and pale and dim in their shrouds of nightly mist; through the Nant Françon gorge, where the faded stars were yet shining in the whitening sky-chasms between the black mountains: so into Bangor, yet asleep, shutterful, uninhabited save by drowsy porters and mechanical guards with half extinguished lanterns.

Then a rush of rail; then daylight on heaving sea and grey sand and windy wood; then Chester, with the purple morning on its orange, crumbling sandstones. And so the day grew bright and glaring and wakeful and old; and station was added to station, and man to man, till nothing but change seemed new in the world.

At length, for even journeys draw to a close, Abraham found himself standing on a lonely station platform in the presence of one porter very much run to dirt, and a ticket-clerk with an obvious and accountable tendency to melancholia, surveying his carpet-bag on the one hand, and the diminishing train "down the line" on the other.

"How am I to get to Hawarden Grange?" said he to the ticket-clerk.

The ticket-clerk looked at the porter, and the porter looked at the ticket-clerk.

Finally the porter remarked that farmer Grillson, who lived about five miles away, used to have a market-cart which he had once lent to a "commercial gent" (with a glance at Abraham's bag) but that last Lady-day the cart had come to grief and had never been repaired.

Apparently ashamed of which feeble observation the speaker retired, possessing himself previously and with a jerk of the passenger's ticket, which the clerk inspected as though it were a novelty, and therefore a nuisance, and retired also.

Abraham mentally used strong language, but at the instant he caught the welcome sound of wheels and the rapid beat of something which was evidently not farmer Grillson's grey and blind old mare. Then a strong man's cheery voice, to whom apparently the ticket-clerk croaked: and presently entered at right door the dingy porter, now obsequious, who, with a scrape at what was once, probably, the site of his leather-cap's rim, announced that "Squire Lee has come for your honour, sir," and forthwith shouldered the neglected carpet-bag and piloted Abraham out of his difficulties.

"Ah," said Mr. Lee, "there you are! Not much luggage, eh? That's right! very glad to see you. Not home yet though, eh? Rather late for the train; never was late for the train in my life before to-day though, eh? In with the carpet-bag, porter! So—so—that's right. Now then, old Trumpeter, fifteen miles in five minutes under the hour. That'll do well enough, Mr. Black, eh? eh?"

And "old Trumpeter" did it easily, helped considerably by the high wheels and light body of Mr. Lee's dog-cart, and the good driving of the old Squire, who never touched his horse with the whip during the whole journey; for, as he observed to Abraham,

"Trumpeter (know why I call him so, Mr. Black, eh? 'cause he blows so—a regular roarer, always was, but does his thirty miles in two hours—good name, eh? eh?) Trumpeter never has had the whip given him ever since I drove him, a matter of ten years, and wouldn't take it now at a gift. Right sort of horse for a country squire, eh? eh? So," he went on, "you're come to take your sister away from us, Mr. Black, eh? Very glad to see you, eh? But think you oughtn't to treat us in that sort of way."

"I am extremely obliged to you, Mr. Lee," began Abraham.

"Eh? Oh!" said Mr. Lee, "I forgot. Nobody within ten miles and more of Hawarden Grange calls me that sort of thing—everybody calls me Squire, eh? Can't say why: but so they do. You do the same, Mr. Black, eh? eh?"

"Well," said Abraham, with a scarcely repressed smile, "if you will allow me at this early stage of our acquaintance to take that liberty, Squire, I am really deeply indebted to you for all your kindness to my sister, who has been your guest for so long a time, and to me, who hardly expected this personal attention of yours on my arrival at the station."

"Eh? The lift? eh? Oh! Of course! Couldn't walk fifteen miles with a carpet-bag. Dare say he could though, eh? Fine, strong, strapping man like that. Fond of hunting, shooting, fishing, farming, or what, Mr. Black? eh? eh? eh?"

"I'm fond of all and each of them, I believe," answered Abraham. "I farm myself, though I dare say you would open your eyes, Mr. Lee—I beg your pardon—at some of our Devonshire proceedings."

"Oh!" laughed Mr. Lee, "yes, to be sure: I know something of Devon farming. Grazing fields full of large banked hedges and small red cattle, eh? Can't grow a decent crop of turnips for love or money or both, eh? eh?"

"Well," said Abraham, "we're learning to do that and to grow mangolds too. I and many of my neighbours shall have fine root crops this year; we're not above improvement."

And so they chatted on their honest country-talk as the road slipped rapidly away under their feet, and the daylight waned.

By-and-bye, at an angle of the road, two tall stone pillars, griffin-crowned, and bearing between them a delicate network of hammered and twisted iron, stood out grimly against the sky-line; and then a long drive through a wooded valley with vanishing glimpses of antlers half-hidden in the dewy fern-brakes; and then a stately whispering avenue of arching limes; and then "welcome to Hawarden," said Mr. Lee, as he pulled up Trumpeter, who hadn't turned a hair, before the great stone porch.

The moon was rising above the hill-tops, and threw the broken outline of the many-gabled grange in a soft flickering shadow on the glittering gravel and velvet lawn. Lights twinkled in the deeply-recessed and mullioned windows; the bell in the eastern turret rang out cheerily, half summons, half welcome. A broad blaze of light flashed across the road as the hall-doors swung back on their heavy hinges, and died away again into still moonlight as the travellers entered, and Trumpeter, nothing loth, was led away by a couple of smart looking grooms to his warm stable.

That evening Abraham found himself one of so cheerful and so picturesque a group in the old grange hall, that as we cannot photograph his pleasant situation, we are tempted to give it somewhat in pen-and-ink detail. The hall was large and lofty, square in shape or nearly so, opening out into the porch, and by many doors into the various rooms adjacent to it. On each side of the main entrance were two large pointed windows with stone mullions and tracery, filled in with stained-glass. Opposite was a long gallery of carved and pierced oak-work. The whole of the walls were panelled in blackest oak, and lit with silver sconces. The roof was open, and elaborately carved and groined. Two huge fireplaces with stone seats in their cavernous recesses came out buttress-fashion into the hall, and even on summer evenings the cheerful crackling leaping blaze of their wood fires was a pleasant companion. A deep soft crimson carpet, and scattered colonies of carved and glistening oak tables, settees, chairs, and ottomans, made the great hall the most cosy and comfortable room in the Grange.

In fact Mr. Lee never could be made to

spend his home evenings elsewhere, and grumbled audibly whenever a gathering of county magnates tied him to the suite of "state apartments," ("all show and gimcracks and no peace and comfort, eh? eh?") conservatory, boudoir, drawing-room, music-room, which opened one into the other on the western side of the house.

So, Abraham not being considered as company, they sat that evening in a snug and happy group round one of the big wood fires; Abraham in the post of honour in a huge oak-chair or throne all over quaint griffins and other unknown monsters, Caroline on a low ottoman at his feet, Amy Lee opposite looking very piquante and loveable in the flickering firelight, Mrs. Lee near her, working quietly and happily, and the old Squire with a favourite dog or two at his feet in the recess of the great chimney, evidently about to light a huge silver-mounted pipe which he was contemplating approvingly before commencing operations.

I don't think they began by talking a great

deal except in a desultory manner; people never do who are perfectly at home with each other, and Abraham generally made himself one of any family party without difficulty, being natural-minded and not given to speculate about the impression he was making.

Presently the Squire said, knocking out the ashes of his first pipe,

"You'd much better stay on with us, Mr. Black, instead of taking your sister away from us: we can't spare her at all, Mrs. Lee, eh? You and I would get on capitally together I see already. Could show you some good coursing. Got a trout-stream, I think. And give you a wrinkle or two in the farming-line, eh? Come now, write to your friend, and tell him to come and join you here: friend of yours, friend of mine, eh? eh? eh?"

And the Squire lit pipe number two to a running accompaniment of his usual encouraging interrogative.

"Really, Mr. Black," began Amy Lee, "it's too bad of you to run away with Caroline just as she is beginning to know the place and to like wandering about with me in all manner of wildernesses ! What am I to do when I am left all alone by myself?" with a pretty air of desolation which Abraham found it hard to resist.

"Well, you see," he said, "we've made our plans, and so I think we must abide by them; though I confess the temptations" (with a half glance at Amy Lee) "to do otherwise are unexpectedly great."

Caroline glanced up at her brother's face rather mischievously, and with one of his hands in hers,

"I don't think you must say too much to us, or I see that Mr. Abey will give in, being properly accustomed to female government, and so I shan't get any trip at all. You know I have set my heart on seeing a mountain, and I've promised Mrs. Lee to come back again to the Grange before very long, and I mean to make Abey come too; so we shall manage both plans capitally."

Mr. Lee chuckled a little to himself.

Said Amy, "I see we have made a small

mistake. We ought to have got Caroline over to our side first, and then have asked Mr. Black afterwards. Do you always do as Caroline bids you, Mr. Black? What a capital brother you must be!"

"Well," answered Abraham, with a laugh, "if Caroline gives me what she thinks is a good character, I suppose I oughtn't to spoil it. You know men always think they have their own way, and I suppose always have it, when possible."

"Quite right," said Mrs. Lee, "we shouldn't enquire too closely into these small home matters; and I dare say Caroline's government is not too despotic to be a pleasant one. But when must you take her away, Mr. Black? She talks about a very early day, which we really cannot allow."

"I am afraid," replied Abraham, "that the day after to-morrow must see us travelling Wales-wards. To-morrow I hope to be lionized by Mr. Lee over his farm and stables and kennels, and by Miss Lee and Caroline over those endless gardens and waste and howling wildernesses of which I have heard so much."

"Now Caroline," interrupted Amy, "I wonder what wonderful tales-out-of-school you have been telling your brother. I am afraid, Mr. Black, you think that your sister has been already too long away from your wise government, and that she and I have been running wild in Staffordshire wildernesses very much to the spoiling of her sedate and quiet manners."

"Well, I don't know," said Abraham, "I dare say she has aided and abetted you ably in every outdoor roving and rambling, and spoiled her best bonnet half-a-dozen times over already, if she ever had such a thing, which I have reasons to doubt."

Abraham received a small sisterly pinch for his speech, and Caroline went on,

"You know, Abey, I told you that I was trying to persuade Amy to join us and nearly succeeded, but we really couldn't get a proper chaperon."

"No," laughed Amy; "the Squire said he

wouldn't go nearer a Welsh mountain than Chester for the world, as he would be sure to break his horse's knees and his own neck, if he got into such foreign countries."

"Very well for you to talk about me, Miss Amy," said the Squire, "but what sort of figure do you think I and Trumpeter would cut climbing up Snowdon together on a broiling hot July afternoon, and how should either of us ever get down again?"

"And," continued Amy, "Mama said she hadn't left the Squire for thirty years, and wouldn't do it now."

"Such is the retentive love of government in the female mind," said Abraham in a *very* inaudible whisper to Caroline, who was half inclined to repeat his remark aloud for Amy's benefit, and didn't do so.

"And," went on Amy, not quite catching the aside, "there was my aunt Elizabeth, who began to bargain for a travelling carriage and a lady's-maid; and there was dear old Miss Prodgers, who would have wanted at least three extra band-boxes for her fronts, and wouldn't have gone at all if she had known that a strange gentleman was to have received us at this place with an unpronounceable name to which you are bound. And as Caroline and I can't go by ourselves, I can't go at all."

"I thought," interrupted Abraham, "that I was such an old and steady and family a man that I might have been entrusted with any number of young ladies. I have chaperoned a great many in my time with much foresight and success."

"I wouldn't trust you now," said Caroline, and "You see it would be Caroline's chaperoning after all, Mr. Black," said Amy, "if you are as well under orders as she says, and I trust you are."

And so chatting idly and chancefully perhaps, as talk goes which after all bears life-fruits neither idly nor chancefully, the evening went away quickly enough; and then Mr. Lee and Abraham were left to enjoy a final pipe of peace; and then there was high sleep in the quiet Grange, whilst the cool moonlight slid from tree to tree, lingering in the dripping fern-copses, gliding up the misty hill-sides, wandering away down distant dewy glades as the dawn rose in gold and amber, and the last weary star paled away in the vivid glare of the open day.

CHAPTER VII.

A CHANCE GUEST.

ALL that day Abraham was trudging sturdily by the Squire's side over fallow, ploughed land, and pasture; now handling fat bullocks, now talking of the rotation of crops, now estimating the marketable value of ricks, stacks, and granaries. Then a long inspection of stables, loose-boxes, summer-runs, kennels, and so forth ensued; and afterwards a ramble with the girls through the gardens, where flowers and fruit grew as of their own accord; and a final wandering through "the wilderness," where the trout lived and rose in the still pools under the fern-banks, and the deer lay lazily in the pleasant shade of oak and beech, heedless and careless of chance footsteps and harmless intrusion.

After a short time Amy Lee quite got rid of any provoking and shy ways in which she at first indulged, and seemed to regard Abraham (much to his pleasure) very much as Caroline did, as a quiet sedate brother, who was to be taken about, and made much of, and asked questions, and generally looked upon as an old and very trustworthy friend.

In fact Abraham and Amy must have liked one another wherever they had met one another, as being both agreed in thinking little of themselves and much of other people, which after all is the secret of naturalness, and the basis of all healthy society, true friendship, and that state of mind and relationship which is not altogether different from socialness and friendship.

In the evening there was a very small dinner-party: the parson of the parish, whom Mr. Lee liked chiefly because he had a capital seat, and nand on, and a good eye for a horse, preached short practical sermons, and knew and liked (more or less) every man, woman, child, and dog in the parish: Miss Prodgers in her newest front, gorgeously dyed (with the exception of the palpable network-parting) of a vivid purple-shining black: and a Mr. Carwithen, who lived some five miles off at Marley Hall, and was a tall thin sallow faced man of any age, with a careworn expression about his eyes, and a slow hesitating way of expressing his opinions, which he never did unless specially called upon so to do.

We need not give the dinner in detail, or the conversation, for we have to get back speedily to Jonas White at Pen-y-gwryd. Only we must record a casual after-dinner talk which occurred between Abraham and Mr. Carwithen, who happened to be near neighbours when the ladies had departed.

"I thought," said Mr. Carwithen, helping himself to claret, and waiting till the operation was performed before he went on with his remark, "I thought I heard you just now speaking to Mr. Lee about a Mr. White, apparently a friend of yours?"

"Yes," said Abraham enquiringly, as Mr. Carwithen appeared to have concluded his conversation, and to be listening to the clergyman and Mr. Lee, who were discoursing parish matters in loud voices, "yes, I have an old friend of that name."

"Ah!" replied Mr. Carwithen, "the name caught my ear. I once too had a friend of the same name. But it can hardly be the same man. Do you know whether your friend comes of a Staffordshire family?"

"No, I think not," answered Abraham, "indeed I am sure he has no connection with this part of the world. His father was a London merchant in very large business, and failed unhappily in the last commercial panic, and Jonas White (my friend) was suddenly reduced from wealth to poverty; and has now to support his mother and sister as well as himself by his own exertions."

"Ah, you interest me," said Mr. Carwithen, very apathetically; "and pray, if I may ask, as a total stranger, how does Mr. White bear his change of life? Such a sudden reverse would sour many a young man."

"But not Jonas White," answered Abraham. "He is just as cheerful, active, and enterprising as in old days; his bright and happy life is even a greater blessing to his family than the money he brings them. And, knowing him most intimately as I do, I have never heard him express one vain regret, or lament for an instant all he has known and lost."

"A brave man," said Mr. Carwithen, in an under-voice. "And has your friend no 'prospects in life?'" he continued.

"Well," said Abraham, "I can't say that he has, except perhaps the prospect of rising to a head-clerkship, when he is grey-headed, in the Bank where he now works."

"Yes," said Mr. Carwithen, in a melancholy tone, "he works on a treadmill with the shadowy improbability of a future overseership in the same institution. Well, but he may marry some day, and retrieve his fortunes by a lucky speculation in the matrimonial market."

Abraham glanced for an instant at the other end of the table, and perceived that the Squire and the clergyman were still in high conversation, and then said,

"I am afraid he has little chance of embarking in any such speculations. You seem to take an interest in the story, and so I may venture to add (in confidence) that my friend's affections seem to be rather hopelessly entangled. In fact he cannot afford to marry as he doubtlessly would; and I know him well enough to be sure that he will never speculate in another direction."

"And is the lady in every respect worthy of him?" asked Mr. Carwithen.

"I am sure of that," replied Abraham shortly, not trusting himself to say more.

"Ah," answered Mr. Carwithen sombrely, "it is the old story, old as life, fools and idiots and incapables prosper in this world and have riches in possession and marry whom they will; whilst the brave and the wise see their fortunes dwindle and their hopes decay. And yet the provision is worthy of the highest system of religion, for a fool in adversity is a spectacle contemptible to God and men, and a wise man in sorrow is a light and a beacon to the whole world."

There was a pause, and then Mr. Carwithen continued, "I thank you for your confidence, Mr. Black. The story is of much interest to me; for I have been young, though now old, and I, from my haven of age, not unblest though crowned with none of the hopes of my early days, can look out with sympathy and admiration on all the early life-struggles of brave and unconquerable men."

And here the Squire interposed with a question on farming matters, and the conversation became general, and there was a speedy adjournment to the ladies in the hall.

Next day with many expressions of regret, and promises to return at the earliest opportunity, Caroline and Abraham took leave of the family at the Grange, and set out on their road to Pen-y-gwryd.

The Squire drove them to the station in great state, turning out for the occasion in his drag with four greys in hand, handling them as if he loved them, which he did. Amy sat on the box-seat beside her father, her own place; and Caroline thought that Abraham's good-bye to her was rather demonstrative for him.

So as they were bowling along in the down-mail somewhere between Chester and Llangollen-road, Caroline, remarking that her brother was rather silent and considerative, said abruptly,

"And what do you think of Amy Lee? You never told me whether you think she comes up to my account of her."

"So you are afraid that you exaggerated your friend's good qualities, are you?" he answered, with a partly-conscious smile.

"That's no answer, Abey," said his sister.

"Well," replied Abraham, "I will give you the benefit of the doubt this time, for really I think she is a very good-tempered 'jolly' girl, as you remarked in your letter, and I think too that there is a great deal more in her than comes out of her in the atmosphere of the Grange."

"Why don't you try and transplant her, Abey?" said Caroline.

This observation was made in an undertone, and Abraham did not seem to have heard it, for he went on looking out of the window, and his next remark was something about telegraph-wires, which was not as interesting a subject to Caroline as if he had vouchsafed to answer her question.

Caroline's delight as the great panorama of Welsh mountains began to open out, when they had passed Corwen and were beginning to near the way-side posting-house of Cerrig-y-druiddion, was very refreshing to Abraham, who like most men never thoroughly enjoyed scenery when alone. Abraham named the principal points, Snowdon and Trifaen as peaks, the rounded summit of Siabod, and the rocky heights of the Glyders.

"Just underneath that craggy Glyder is Pen-y-gwryd; I hope that will be sufficiently 'mountaineous' for you, Caroline?".

"Yes, I think it looks very hopeful," said Caroline, with a bright gleam in her eyes, and then she added, "I wonder why a great panorama of mountains like this is so pleasant to look at?"

"Why," laughed Abraham, "that is just the sort of question which Jonas is always asking me; you and he together would drive a humble-minded philosopher to his wits' ends. I think, for one thing, one experiences the same sort of pleasure which one feels in looking at a well-executed map. One gets a general notion of the 'lie' of the country; and mentally fills up the detail in accordance with one's previous knowledge of nature. Here one discovers a windy pass, there a deep and sombre spur-valley, there a lonely peak, sun-jewelled, or mist-wreathed, or snow-hidden. Here must be a sparkling lake, there the course of a leaping mountain stream. And so one's imagination is set to work to realise details, and the more one knows of nature in small matters the more one likes to look at her outspread panoramas.

"Then,—for this might apply to any description of natural panorama,—with regard to distant views of mountains, one has an inborn longing for high-lands. Men and women are more or less demoralized in lowlands, partly perhaps from the effects of atmosphere, but chiefly because one has an instinct which may be characterised as non-stationary.

"A man, a true man, is not content with the knowledge that is, he craves to grasp a knowledge to be. Columbus craved to know what was beyond the echoing waves of the trackless Atlantic; Franklin, to penetrate the silent Arctic seas; Livingstone, to map out the vast unknown of Africa. A happy *valley* is an impossibility; a man must in time be miserable therein, if he had not climbed the heights and penetrated the regions beyond. One must know what is beyond. These mountains are, obviously, in their simplest aspect, barriers to knowledge; consequently, one surmounts them."

"But couldn't one get round them?" suggested Caroline.

"No; it wouldn't be the same thing. One sees more and more truly from great heights, both physical and moral. A man, you see, does not explore merely to catalogue, he explores to generalize. Now one can't generalize rapidly in a marsh, for one can't see more than half-a-mile ahead in any direction. On a mountain the generalization is ready to hand."

"But Columbus, Livingstone, and the rest, did not particularly aim at mountains?"

"No; their extending journeyings gave them the power of generalizing. I mean one does it at once, as far as geography is concerned, on the top of a mountain."

That night the moon shone dreamily on the high mountains as they drew near Pen-y-gwryd. Here a peak gleamed like a star; there a mountain-side slept in calmest shadow; now a lake loomed mistily in a low valley; now a stream sparkled in rippling lines of silver on the far hill-side. There was no sound but the sound of many waters, and the rush of the wandering night-wind, and the tramping of the horses' feet. Presently there were lights; and the deep barking of dogs; and then the voice of Jonas White.

"So you're come, and well-come, at last! We had given you up for to-night. I am delighted to see the arrival! A three-days' solitude in a solitary place is a sufficient expiation for the crimes of the last three months. Now, Harry Bach,* bring the lantern and light the lady out of the car! Sharp is the word!"

And so with a shower of words and immense bodily exercise in the way of shouldering luggage, wraps, and what-not, Jonas successfully accomplished the task of getting over his first interview with the required balance of nonchalance and heartiness.

There was high supper on oat-cakes and porter; and much talk, chiefly about Hawarden, Pen-y-gwryd being reserved by mutual

---

* "Bach"—*ch* guttural and unpronounceable by English throats.

consent for the next morning; and then to bed, with the cheerful prospect of a fortnight's pleasant rambling on the mountain by way of subject for quiet dreams in time present and time future.

CHAPTER VIII.

PEN-Y-GWRYD.

"ONE great advantage which Pen-y-gwryd has over other abiding-places in North Wales," said Jonas to Caroline next morning at breakfast, "is the inn thereof. The history of an inn is that of a nation."

"Now," laughed Abraham, "we are going to have a philosophical discussion at breakfast. That is really too bad of you, Jonas!"

"Please to go on, Mr. White," said Caroline, "I have a great anxiety to know the history of Pen-y-gwryd, and if it is to be very learned, why you know I am not obliged to understand it."

"I mean," said Jonas, "that a nation begins its life obscurely and sordidly, its numbers are few, its location 'remote, unfriended,' 'melancholy' probably, 'slow' without doubt; in like manner was Pen-y-gwryd 'Hotel' six-and-twenty years ago, a wayside cottage on a lonely mountain track, of little importance or use to any but its unimportant occupant. But as time goes on the young nation extends its roots downwards and its branches upwards; it builds cities, fortifications, ships; it raises armies; it cultivates knowledge scientific and artistic: and so it makes progress till the history of its rise culminates in the epoch when though still outwardly prosperous it is inwardly rotting away by reason of what most men call over-civilization, which Abraham there would more justly term a morbid development of the same."

"Hear!" cried Abraham, helping himself to a fresh relay of eggs and " chigmochyn,"* "it's always refreshing to hear oneself quoted

---

* Anglicè, fried ham, a standing dish at Pen-y-gwryd, and "no that bad."

by an orator on his legs. By the way, Jonas, I trust you are not as hungry as I am; for this is evidently your exordium, and as you have been theorizing on Pen-y-gwryd for three whole solitary days, your remarks are evidently 'to be continued' indefinitely."

Jonas (not at all heeding the interruption, and with much earnestness—all his theorizing was in earnest). " But, mark you, that epoch of decay need not, as I believe, ever arrive in the history of any nation; and never does arrive till the nation becomes artificial at the expense of its own historical and race-born nature; when it builds houses and cities not because such things are absolutely needed, but because they make a fair-seeming pomp; when it colonizes not because there is a surplus population, but because there is a craving for change and acquisition; when it throws aside its own specific character, say that of a nation of explorers and merchants, and takes (say) to standing armies on an ever increasing scale, for the sake of excitement, change, or show, then is the end approaching, but, I take it, however much things may prosper, not till then.

"A nation, from this point of view, is not unlike a railway train; once run it off its own line of rails, and destruction and death ensue as a matter of ordinary calculation."

"I think I understand all this," said Caroline, smiling at Jonas's increasing warmth, but how are you going to connect it with Pen-y-gwryd? Is Mr. Henry Owen about to colonize the Glyders with Harry Bach, and form the rest of his family into a model Zouave corps? Mrs. Owen in full Zouave costume would hardly be picturesque."

Abraham exploded, "'Colonize the Glyders with Harry Bach!' A grand expression, Caroline, worthy of Jonas himself! I believe after all it's this newly-built coffee-room, the only tolerably-sized room in the house, which excites his indignation. Something wrong probably about the carpet or the curtains. Not sufficiently Chevreul-esque for his professorship. Now Jonas, what is it? The audience waits impatiently but humbly to receive light."

Jonas. "A moral to an allegory is always dull. You should apply a fable for yourselves. And in this case the interest lies chiefly in the allegory. But *in re* Pen-y-gwryd I think a far-seeing inn-keeper in North Wales would not improve his house beyond a certain point. There are so many civilized hotels for civilized tourists. We quiet people want a quiet house in a quiet spot. We come to Pen-y-gwryd chiefly because we find here what we want. White-throated waiters and cherry-ribboned chambermaids are abominations to me, and many other men. Let there be such things for the thorough-going tourist who requires such things even on a Welsh mountain, but do not rob the plain traveller of his plain inn.

"I have been endeavouring to impress these views on our landlord, with but small success —he being ambitious and aspiring. If I come here for my sins twenty years hence I shall find a French cook, a staff of London-bred servants, and a Salon à la Louis Quatorze, and then Pen-y-gwryd will be an abomination in the eyes of all right-minded men.

"By the way, Abraham, you've not seen our photographic establishment. Come and see it. You must have had enough breakfast to last for a week.

"Let me introduce you, Miss Black, to our sanctum."

Jonas had persuaded Mrs. Owen, in one of her weaker moments, to give him undisturbed possession of one of her smaller bed-rooms. He had made a grand clearance of furniture; nailed yellow calico over the windows; erected "Judy" by way of a dark cupboard in which to dry his plates; and constructed a laboratory-table of her packing-case. There was a chaos of bottles, and a consuming odour of chemicals, and divers spots and stains about a floor which was once scrupulously stainless.

"Couldn't do this in a fashionable hotel," said Jonas in triumph.

"And what do Pen-y-gwryd visitors in general say to your proceedings?" asked Caroline, when Abraham had given his unqualified approbation of the arrangements.

"Why," said Jonas, "I fancy I am a public

nuisance. Two elderly ladies with a small waggon-load of shining boxes, well corded, cased, and labelled after the manner of women, arrived here two days ago with a crinolined lady's-maid and a shucky lap-dog. The whole party made a dead point at the door of this room, wherein I happened to be working. They sniffed a good deal. Then the lady's-maid cried, 'Well, I never! Ow orrid!' and the ladies murmured inarticulately and not amiably; and finally they went into an apparently endless controversy with the landlady. I opened a bottle of collodion, and lit a pipe, which necessarily brought matters to a crisis. And I am happy to say that these tourists are now sojourning at the Hotel of Capel Curig, where I have no intention of molesting them."

Abraham. "Jonas's theory of civilization, taking form in Jonas's practice is possibly questionable. And what results have you to show for your general unpleasantness?"

Jonas. "O, here are half-a-dozen or so respectable negatives. Here's a view of Pen-y-gwryd which is more truthful than picturesque. But the best news of all is that the stream at the back of the house, which comes down from Llyn-y-cwm-ffynon, is as good as distilled water for all our purposes—no more iron and lake-debris as at Tal-y-llyn to worry us. If photographers only knew this we should have an establishment in every bedroom, and be obliged to bivouac on the mountain in self-defence.

"And now I beg humbly to propose that Miss Black puts on her bonnet, and Abraham gets his rod together, and that I escort the whole party to Llyn-y-cwm-ffynon, where I have some big stones to show Abraham, about which I have no doubt he will know quite as much as he did about his volcano on Cader; moreover Miss Black may go a-ferning to her heart's content, and Abraham may flog the lake till his patience is exhausted and his basket as empty as when he began."

"Well," said Abraham, "that is a cheerful programme for me at all events! But we may as well go, for it will be a shame to lose this glorious morning, and one water is as good as another in the present parched and fiery state of things."

So they set off, clambering up the hill-side to the north-west of Pen-y-gwryd; now and then plashing through soft boggy ground which no heat was able to dry up.

"That's what I call a sensible get-up for mountain or country-side, Caroline!" said Abraham admiringly, as with the aid of a light iron-shod ashen pole she held her way with the stronger climbers. "Capital boots those, with the light steel nails; and proper heels too, I see! Then you have evidently no exo-skeleton either of whalebone above or steel below. The woollen dress and petticoat are cool, and they wont tear. And the grey hat without feathers and danglers is as good a shade as any wide-awake."

"Yes," said Caroline, looking much prettier than ever, flushed as she was with exercise and healthy excitement, "I knew that you two long-legged persons meant work, and that if I was not to be a nuisance to you I must work too, and so I thought I had better dress myself accordingly. Miss Prodgers in crinoline and tight-fitting wig would never have risen twenty feet above the inn."

In a quarter of an hour they were looking down on the lake, a small sheet of shallow water in an angle of one shoulder of the Glyder Vawr. Its shores to the West were low and marshy; to the East rocky and broken.

"Now, Miss Black," said Jonas, "amongst these crags you and I will go fern-hunting if you please, while Abraham vainly endeavours to catch some of the excellent trout with which the lake abounds."

"Very well, Mr. White," replied Caroline demurely, "since you are so very polite as to offer me your escort I shall have much pleasure in availing myself of that advantage."

And as they scrambled on together she added, "I really think that in this wild part of the world we might as well put off other formalities with our crinolines and Sunday-going coats; and as I hereby authorize you to call me Caroline, so I intend to read Jonas for

Mr. White—until we arrive at some civilized town, Welsh, or otherwise, where there are at least gas-lights and a pavement."

"Ah," said unfortunate Jonas, not venturing to show a tithe of the pleasure he felt at this sudden arrangement or of the qualms with which he accepted that which he could not reject, "that is a capital idea of yours, for if we are to enjoy ourselves we may as well do it thoroughly, without buckram and starch. And," he added, by way of salve to his conscience, "as Abraham has been a brother of mine for so long, his sister ought to be mine too."

"You haven't said 'Caroline,' yet, Jonas!"

"There!" said Jonas, getting wonderfully red in the face and making a frantic dive into a rock-chasm, from which he emerged with a bunch of fern in his hand, "there is a prize for you, Caroline, no less than the Parsley-fern,* which I don't fancy you have yet added to your collection."

---

* *Allosorus crispus.*

Caroline took it from him with many thanks, wondering a little to herself at Jonas's sudden excitement and his rather unusual shyness.

This latter state of mind, however, soon wore off, as the clambering and hunting went on; during which Jonas took so much unnecessary care of his companion that she at last laughingly remonstrated, asking whether he thought her quite incapable of getting over a six-inch stone without his able-bodied assistance.

Between them they made a very fair botanical haul that morning; there were seven or eight different species of ferns,* among them the memorable Allosorus aforesaid, and no less than five different Lycopodiums, *cla-*

---

* *J. W.*—1. Male-fern,
        2. Ditto, var. Borreri,
        3. Common polypody,
        4. Hard-fern,
        5. Lastræa dilatata,
        6. Ditto, var. dumetorum,
        7. Parsley-fern.

vatum, selago, selaginoides, alpinum, and *inundatum.*

"And," said Jonas, as they counted up their treasures in a shady nook of the rocks, "I've got four or five more ferns to give you, which I gathered the day before you came in a certain wild place called Clogwyn-y-cwscua, half way up the Nant Gwynant pass. There were '*ruta muraria,*' *adiantum nigrum, a. trichomanes,* and higher up the mountain I found lots of '*viride.*' And now let's sit down here a little longer and wait for Abraham, whose patience is greater than Job's,— who, by the way, never had that useful quality tried by the severest of tests, a summer-day's fly-fishing on a Welsh lake during dry weather.

So they sat down and waited in the cool shade; Caroline in a dry mossy niche of the rock, with her hat at her feet, round which she had twisted a pretty wreath of Lycopodium; Jonas leaning against the entrance with her alpen-stock in his hand, thinking fragmentary thoughts about Oreads, and not in truth admiring the landscape as much as he might have done.

There was a blazing cloudless sun in mid-sky, in whose light the rock-strewn mountains were flashing and quivering with a strange unearthlike tremulousness. A little stream was tinkling shrilly in an unseen valley: and now and then a stray stone or a tiny avalanche of debris would rattle down the mountain-side as the wandering sheep moved lazily in search of fresh pasture.

Presently there was a great commotion and lifting up of voices among the mountain flock.

"What can be the matter with those sheep?" asked Caroline, as the cry became universal.

Jonas woke up to a sense of things external, and looked out in the direction of the noise; at length he said, "Quite quietly! Come out, and stand by me."

There were two magnificent Peregrine falcons in full adult plumage, circling round a neighbouring mound, and every now and then uttering a shrill cry, which the sheep had heard and were re-echoing with every variety of intonation.

"What glorious birds!" said Caroline, who had never seen one before in its full life and power.

By-and-bye they settled on the mound, moving backwards and forwards and preening their shining feathers in the full sun-blaze.

"Let me shout!" said Jonas, who would have given all the ferns in Wales at that moment for his rifle; and he raised a prolonged Australian 'Coo-e-e-e' which effectually drove the Peregrines from their castle, and with a few graceful curves and circles they swept over the hill-side and were lost to sight.

Then the shout seemed to find a dilatory echo in the direction of the lake, and presently came up the patient Abraham, very hot, and very thirsty, and very fishless.

"I renounce Welsh fishing in broiling July," said he as he threw himself down in the shade at Caroline's feet, "and humbly beg the pardon of my own despised little trout-stream at home, for preferring a shallow blazing Welsh puddle to its cool shady rock-pools."

"I don't see, though," said Jonas, "why you should abuse Llyn-y-cwm-ffynon, seeing that all those speedily-devoured breakfast-trout of ours came out of its shallows."

"Latched,* I suppose," answered Abraham indignantly.

"I fancy you're not so far wrong," laughed Jonas. "But now, Abraham, I'll console you. Here is what I wanted to show you. What is your opinion of *that!*" laying his hand on the scarped cliff beside him.

"Why," said Caroline, "it's a common bit of stone, with not even a fern upon it."

Abraham looked up lazily at the place indi-

---

* The Latch is a Welsh institution much employed by hotel-caterers. It is simply a flat board, with a sail of some description attached to it; it carries a long line hung with flies across a lake, and speedily ensures a good dish of fish. As however many more fish are pricked than caught, the survivors are rendered wary, and the fisherman-sportsman indignant.

cated; "I can't see," he said, "for your hand,"—which Jonas moved.

Then with a sudden bound—to Caroline's great surprise—he leapt up crying, "glacier striations, by Jupiter! Any more about here, Jonas?"

"Yes," said Jonas, "thanks to Professor Ramsay's Welsh paper and map in 'peaks, passes, and glaciers,' I have been working up the subject with much success; and though there are abundance of striæ both behind and in front of Pen-y-gwryd, I brought you up here first because the markings on this angle of rock are easily accessible, and are close to a fine series of blocs perchés on the hill above; and moreover that by a slight clamber we can get on to the side of Llanberis Pass, where the tracks of the glacier lie in every direction, and are of every description, striæ, mammillations or roches moutonnées, blocs perchés, and moraines; and where you may theorize to your heart's content."

"O," cried Caroline, "*if* you please! Will you have pity on the ignorance of the female mind in general, and mine in particular? What are all these dreadful words of all manner of foreign languages in which you have been indulging, and why should they come up to the top of a Welsh mountain?"

"If you wish for a lecture on the subject," said Jonas, "you have only to set Abraham and me agoing, and I have no doubt that between us you will get as complicated and confused an idea on the subject of the last Welsh novelty as you can possibly desire."

"—— Caroline. If you please," said that young woman.

"Well, Caroline, if you please," said he.

"But first of all," added, Abraham, who had made a brief inspection of the neighbouring rocks in the meanwhile, "let us look at these 'perched blocks' and then sit down somewhere on the side of the big Pass, and I'll give you my ideas and Jonas shall give you his, and you may doze undisturbedly during the process without injuring the *amour propre* of either of us."

"But first of all," said Caroline, "show

me what Jonas has shown you, and what you have been good enough to call a glacial striation."

Abraham. "Why, don't you see that this rock is polished, and has one or two deep grooves cut in it, which grooves don't follow the stratification—"

"O!" said Caroline.

Abraham. "Well, the ordinary cleavage— the ordinary direction of the grain of the rock —but follow the direction of the valley— which is supposed to have been caused by the down-pressing action of a big glacier, whose imprisoned stones would naturally make such a mark as this in an opposing rock."

"But," objected Caroline, "why couldn't something else have made this mark? Why a glacier, this not being Switzerland?"

"What else could?" said Abraham, "this is an exact copy of a Swiss-glacier mark; neither fire nor water action could produce such a mark. Fire would split stone, water would round and smooth it. Only an angular rock enclosed in a sliding glacier could gouge out this clean-cut impression. No other known action except that of an ancient glacier could accomplish this result, and therefore we may justly suppose a glacier to have been its cause."

Then leaving fishing-rods and other impediments behind, they climbed the mountain-side, skirting the shoulder of the Glyder Vawr; and by-and-bye Jonas cried,

"There! look there!—on the tops and sides of those rounded hills! There is a regular line, a quarter of a mile or more in length, of isolated massive stones. There is no cliff in the neighbourhood from which they could fall; there is nothing to *stop* them here, if they had been hurled along in the swoop of a mighty deluge; if they had been deposited ordinarily by water they would have been sorted according to weight, and would have been rounded like torrent or sea-side pebbles. What then can be plainer than that they were dropped quietly, one by one, as a large glacier which filled this valley melted slowly in the lapse of unnumbered years? And similarly these rounded hills are, plainly, not shaped by water, which would have left distinctly-cut chasms, ravines, and water-courses, but are made by the even, gradual friction of the under surface of slowly-moving ice-masses."

In half an-hour's time they were perched on a stray boulder, looking down on the Pass of Llanberis.

"I think," said Caroline, "that we ought to be very much obliged to people who open our eyes for us. What a wonderful deal of extra pleasure one gets by knowing ever so little out of the evident present of things which surround us. I shall never be grateful enough to Ruskin, whose 'Modern Painters' made me first notice clouds and water. And now these mountains no longer rock-strewn and fern-covered are beginning to glisten with grinding ice and to be crowned with eternal snow."

Abraham. "So that Wales plus the glacier theory equals Switzerland minus the nuisance of a rough channel-passage."

Jonas. "Now, Abraham, be kind enough to chew the cud of your glacial studies. I know that you possess a perfectly endless stock of ice theories: let us have a few of them whilst I light the pipe of attention and Caroline goes on with her crochet. What? No work in that elaborate basket, nothing but sandwiches? Ah! not so good a shot as might have been expected!" dexterously avoiding a small pebble, and coiling himself up comfortably on an adjacent boulder.

"Now," said Abraham, "I call that too bad of you to let me in for a lecture on such a broiling afternoon. But I'll tell Caroline if she likes what little I know about glaciers, premising that I got my information mostly at second-hand in a very clear and useful condensation, which I lit upon in one of the chapters of Mr. Wills' interesting 'Wanderings among the High Alps.'

"There are five main theories which have been successively adopted as explanations of the various phenomena of glaciers: and if we find that many and hard words have been used to explain a now easily-understood process, we must remember that knowledge is of slow growth, and that to the first observers of glaciers little was plain but the seeming changelessness of a vast mass of hard ice.

"One knows now that a glacier is an ice-river, that no portion of it is ever truly stationary: the point to be discussed is the method of and the laws which govern its action.

"Now first there was the 'gravitation theory' upheld by De Saussure, who enunciated the following law :—' A glacier is a body essentially rigid and inflexible, which slides along its channel simply in virtue of its own weight.'

"What would be your objection to that remark, Jonas?"

Jonas. "Why, seeing that a glacier is always on an incline, of course the mass of such a rigid body would be always increasing in velocity. Down a very sudden incline it would let go its hold and become an avalanche: illustration, a block of iron sliding in a long wooden groove."

Abraham. "Good. Then we have the 'dilatation theory' proposed by Charpentier.

This recognises the fact that glacier ice is traversed by capillary fissures and air cavities which become filled by day with surface water. Then the water parts with its heat at night, becomes ice, and expands. Wherefore the glacier proceeds slowly in the direction of the least resistance, that is to say, down-hill. Objections, Jonas?"

Jonas. "Don't know enough of glaciers to make any objections. Will take in the dilatation theory humbly if you like."

Abraham. "Why, Professor Forbes proves that cold retards and heat accelerates glacier movements. Moreover the alteration in glacier temperature is entirely superficial, and therefore would not affect the motion of the underlying mass.

"Next there comes the 'expansion theory' of Mr. Mosely—relying on the ordinary law of expansion among solids, and quoting a sheet of lead on Bristol Cathedral which descended by alternate expansion and contraction eighteen inches in two years. Any objection, Jonas?"

Jonas. "Oh! Ah! Why, I suppose such expansion and contraction produced by alternate day heat and night cold would be merely superficial also."

Abraham. "And next we have Professor Forbes' 'viscous theory.' The Professor says that 'a glacier is an imperfect fluid, or a viscous body, and is urged down slopes of a certain inclination by the mutual pressure of its parts'—which theory is illustrated by Stockholm pitch, a substance capable of slowly descending an incline by its own weight, even when sufficiently solid to allow of its being broken by a hammer; also by a mixture of glue and plaster of Paris, which is made to descend an inclined plane and form casts whose sections are perfect models of those of a natural glacier."

Jonas. "So for the future then instead of saying 'as solid as a lump of ice,' I shall have to observe, 'as sticky as a lump of ice,' and stand up for Professor Forbes against all comers, till the next professor comes."

Abraham. "The next, and latest professor,

Professor Tyndall, enunciates his natural theory which refuses to acknowledge viscosity as a property of ice, and asserts that glacier progress depends upon the result of the perpetual warfare which is going on in the frozen mass between the forces of gravity and cohesion, the latter property being aided by the known power of ice to re-freeze and re-unite when broken, at a comparatively high temperature. The ice-mass, in fact, is not sticky: but it bends till it breaks: the central and superior portion is then freed and advances till it is re-united by freezing to the whole mass at a point lower down the valley: and so the process, endlessly repeated, produces the result for which we have to account."

Jonas. "On the whole I prefer the ultimate to the penultimate professorial theory; for, taking the words in their ordinary acceptation, ice is not viscous, and it is fragile. But, talking of professors, I'll tell you what Professor Ramsay says about this Llanberis Pass, promising (in a parenthesis of amiability) to make Caroline a pretty glacier-model of glue and plaster, by way of improving her mind at the earliest opportunity."

Caroline. "Jonas, I'm not going to be teased and I don't know that I shall accept your present; so you had better go on with your scientific remarks, and I can have a quiet nap in the meanwhile if I like, and feel sleepy."

Jonas (in an oratorical attitude). "The mind of woman is fearfully and wonderfully made. At one time it sympathises with the frailties and encourages the aspirations of the ruder sex; at another time if Homer nod, it denudes him of his night-cap and insists upon his swallowing his gruel, whilst should he be inclined to thunder, it takes away and locks up his chemicals and loses the key on purpose."

Caroline. "Abraham, I vote that you and I go home and leave this rude and ignorant orator to harangue the rocks and the sheep."

Jonas threw himself down on the grass with unnecessary violence. Then he added, "And how do you know that I was not first going to prove the direct contrary of that proposition, and then after the time-honoured fashion of a taking 'leader' to connect the apparently extraneous subject of female perfection with the results of glacier action in Llanberis Pass? I'm an ill-used and maligned individual: that's what I am."

Caroline. "Now go on, Jonas, with the Pass, and don't talk nonsense."

Jonas. "Ah! I suppose it is as well to succumb at once. Well, then, Professor Ramsay believes that Snowdon peak was the centre point of six big glaciers; itself, of course, being eternally snow-crowned. There was the glacier of Cwm Brwynog, the valley which one ascends in climbing Snowdon from Llanberis; then, as we clamber round the mountain from west to east come the glaciers of Cwm Clogwyn, of Cwm Llan, Cwms Llydaw and Dyli, Cwm Glas and Cwm Glas Bach; these two latter debouched into the largest glacier of all, that which filled this Llanberis valley to a depth of from 1,100 to 1,300 feet. Probably, he adds, at one period when the glacier descended into Llanberis Lakes, great icebergs, boulder-laden, floated about in those waters, and deposited their rocky burdens which are even now visible at the bottom of the lakes in calm weather. On either side of this long valley, from where we stand as far down as Llyn Padern and even lower, are unmistakeable striæ—in vast abundance. Blocks of felspathic porphyry, carried from the higher mountains, lie scattered about Llyn Peris. Higher up are erratic boulders with moraine debris. A great moraine bars the entrance to Cwm Glas, opposite the so-called Cromlechs, which are nothing but blocks of stone fallen from the hill-side. And so, all up the Pass, one meets with roches moutonnées, blocs perchés, moraines, and striæ—till the accumulated evidence must at last satisfy the most incredulous mind."

Caroline. "What a grand country this must have been in those old days! And how long ago was it since Wales had all this wealth of ice to show?"

Jonas. "That, to me, is the most astonishing part of the theory. He thinks from various circumstances with which I will not bore you (for you should read his own awakening paper in his own simple words) that 'the eyes of men may have looked upon the Welsh glaciers, when, in their latter days, the ice had shrunk far up into the highest recesses of the mountains.' And I presume he accepts the ordinary computation of the age of the human race, and does not adopt Baron Bunsen's theory, which places the birth of the first man at a distance of 26,000 years from that of my friend Abraham."

Abraham. "Thank you, Jonas. Your lecture is more interesting than mine; and you have the further advantage of illustrating your subject with diagrams which even time itself seems impotent to efface."

Eventful as was our little party's daily life at Pen-y-gwryd during the cloudless weather which made their stay resemble one long happy summer's afternoon, one must not, with the fear of the "courteous reader" before one's eyes, attempt more than a slight sketch of its pursuits and pleasures. The rods were speedily laid aside as next to useless, even in the lakes; but the cameras were always rambling about, now climbing the steeps of Cwm Dyli, with its endless succession of flashing waterfalls; now wandering about the chaotic wilderness of Llanberis Pass; now making longer and no less interesting excursions which we shall briefly record in an ensuing chapter.

Every night chemicals were in the (inn) ascendant, until Jonas drying his plates by the kitchen fire somewhere about the small hours, and Abraham washing his cloths and dishes in the neighbouring Gwryd at early dawn, seemed a natural part and parcel of the great Pen-y-gwryd Institution.

Then for Jonas and Abraham there was vast matutinal splashing in a fairly deep pool of the Gwryd not far from the bridge, though from the long prevalence of scorching weather it must be confessed that the pool water was not of the clearest, and that the bathers emerged with a dingy superstratum of moorland debris which was more harmless than becoming.

The botanical boxes too were never idle, and the following brief catalogue of plants may not be unacceptable to any reader who finds himself at any time in the same situation. In Nant Gwynant are *Parnassia palustris, Achillœa ptarmica, Lobelia Dortmanni.* Near Rhaidr-y-Dyli, *Habenaria bifolia* (white butterfly orchis), *Wahlenbergia hederacea* (not a common plant, but plentiful both in Cwm Dyli, and on the banks of the Gwryd), *Orchis latifolia*, a white variety of *Anagallis tenella* (which is found also in Llanberis Pass): and in Clogwyn-y-cwscua, above mentioned, grows *Rhodiola rosea* (a large stone-crop with scented roots), and *Sedum Telephium.*

Jonas, and his "state of mind," seemed to improve wonderfully as time went on. He seldom availed himself of Abraham's recommendation to take strong exercise as a cure for his maladies. When he did so he generally indulged in a constitutional up the Glyder, which as he remarked was enough to "take the nonsense out of any man," and resulted practically in a vast extra consumption of trout, mountain mutton, oat-cakes, and porter. It must be confessed, however, that Caroline's habit of treating him as a big brother whose business of life it was to take care of her on every occasion, and to fetch and carry for her whatever she chanced to want, was considerably trying to his strong-made resolutions— for "resolutions" he read "Balmorals," in alluding to the performance of the many labours of love which he daily underwent in the most willing and uncomplaining of manners. It was always "O Jonas, do carry my big stick and sketch book," or "do lead my pony round this uncomfortable point of rock for me," or "please to stand by that stone in a picturesque attitude while I get in the outlines of this bit of mountain;" and, whether these services were exacted unthinkingly or no, the fact remained that Jonas became so accustomed to render them, that he dared not think of the day when Pen-y-gwryd should know his face no more, and he be separated from Caroline and her many wants once and for ever.

CHAPTER IX.

EXCURSIONIZING.

It was not the least amusing part of the day's work at Pen-y-gwryd to watch in the early morning coach from Pen-y-gwryd, as it rattled down the steep mountain-road from Pen Pass, laden with tourists of every description, and drew up with vast clatter and importance at the inn door. Down scrambles the red-faced cwrw-drinking coachman with a greasy bag of letters in his hand, or a greasier packet in the crown of his ancient wide-awake. Down scramble half-a-dozen many-coloured tourists, some sensibly arrayed in old easy-fitting shooting-jackets and flannels, others primly frock-coated, round-hatted, absurdly "respectable:" away they rush into Mrs.

Owen's sanctum, where the gurgle of the porter tap is heard, and matutinal pipes are set agoing with great unanimity. Then four be-crinolined ladies of certain ages are extracted from the interior of the coach, with that peculiar expression of mixed discomfort and dignity about them which is peculiar to the British elderly female of the middle class on its travels. A merciless swinging, heaving, and crashing of carefully corded and swathed boxes ensues; and then the "Cambrian High-flyer" creaks and groans down the stony road towards Capel Curig, as a tortoise would rattle his slow-going shell against the stones of a dried sea-beach, and as though hurry and speed were always synonymous terms.

On one occasion as Jonas, Abraham, and Caroline were seated in a row on the low wall opposite the inn door inspecting such a scene as the foregoing, there was a Pen-y-gwryd arrival which excited their curiosity and admiration to no small extent.

The arrival was obviously a gentleman, say from 28 to 30 years of age, who was engaged in doing North Wales as thoroughly and perfectly as it could be done according to what Jonas subsequently called his "limited lights." He was regardless of expense but not of appearance. He was dressed in a tawny-grey suit—light cap, shooting-coat, waistcoat, trousers, and gaiters to match—all faultlessly fitting his tall, well-made figure. His Balmorals were serviceable and unimpeachable. His neckerchief was a simple strip of black ribbon, tied loosely on a peculiarly neat "all-rounder." His whiskers and moustache and glossy beard were well-kept, and by no means unmanly. He carried a double-barrelled (not rifle but) opera glass in a white leather case across one shoulder. He was smoking a crookedly twisted cigar, the appearance and savour of which told tales of a running account at Hudson's or Benson's. His luggage was one small black shining portmanteau, undirected, and one walking-stick, a yellowish sapling of an orange or lemon tree, matching as nearly as might be the prevailing tone of his dress.

He was both good-looking, and good-tempered looking, and there was an easy-ful expression in his face, and a certain dimness and fullness of complexion which showed that he was not one of the " mountaine men who for hard livinge toyle," or had ever been accustomed to stint himself of anything that he might happen to want.

Said Caroline, as he got deliberately off the coach, paid the coachman with an air of careless magnificence, and walked into the inn as though it had been erected for his own special use and accommodation, "I feel dreadfully curious to know the name and antecedents of that splendidly-neat tourist."

Jonas (tersely). " Swell, name probably Smith."

Abraham. " Name, Reginald Montgomery Fitz-Urse, youngest son of Sir Walter Fitz-Urse, of Bruinden Castle, Northumberland; occupation, clerk in the treasury; income, above the average of that of his friends; debts, ditto; intellect, tolerable; self-assurance, intolerable."

Caroline. "Not at all a bad guess, Abey, that, I say; though slightly severe, for you. Oh, do look! He is coming out again, and— yes!—he is really going to have the goodness to favour us natives with the light of his patronage. Oh, what fun!"

And she suddenly became quite sedate and demure, as with a calm and undisturbed air, "the Swell," as he was henceforth to be called, strolled leisurely across the road, and slightly lifting his cap as an acknowledgment of Caroline's presence, observed,

"Ar, I find we are fellow-touwists in this pawt of the world. Pen-y-gaw-wed; a good centwal station for Snowdon, I believe, is it not? Clevaw people come to Pen-y-gaw-wed I hear, people who wite?"

"Yes," said Abraham, with preternatural gravity and politeness, "I believe this little inn is the best point in the district for thoroughly seeing the Snowdon country: and Mr. Owen's visitors'-book contains some names very well known in the literary world, whose owners probably would endorse my opinion."

"Ar," said "the Swell," turning towards Caroline with obvious admiration to Jonas' intense indignation, "litewawy people are vewy wefweshing to meet with, that is at fashionable weunions and when they do not woar disagweeably. And can you tell me why this Pen-y-gaw-wed pwopwietor has a yellow window over his fwont door?"

"Oh," laughed Caroline, feeling the relief to be necessary, "that is our photographing room. My brother and his friend work in that room daily."

"Weally!" replied "the Swell," blandly, "Photogwaphy is a vewy intewesting pursuit. I once invested in a camewa myself."

Jonas was on the point of breaking out with a very forcible remark, when "the Swell" again raised his cap to Caroline, and with a slight circumambient bow to the party on the wall, strolled away with leisurely calmness, and was seen no more for the day.

Jonas rushed frantically off the wall, and dashing into the house, confronted Mrs. Owen crying, "Mrs. Owen, who is that man in the yellow-grey clothes, and what is his name, and what does he want here?"

"'Deed and I don't know, sir, I'm sure," said Mrs. Owen with a good-tempered laugh, "he's taken a bed-room for a week, sir, and didn't give his name. He seems a very pleasant, civil-spoken gentleman indeed, sir."

Jonas, muttering thunderously, resought his party, and communicated the intelligence, proposing that they should carry on a photographic operation in "the Swell's" bed-room during his absence, and was only pacified by being carried away in Mr. Owen's car, camera and all, on a long-promised excursion.

They drove first to Capel Curig, pausing at the inn door to admire a procession of two magnificent tourists, gorgeously arrayed in two bran new suits of shining-grey cloth; they were brothers, each the double of the other, six feet high, erect, rejoicing: they "walked in beauty" side by side, the left shoulder of the one and the right shoulder of the other bearing new and shining lake-rods of portentous length. A huge and very new opera-glass dangled between them.

"They have no fishing-basket," said Jonas, "which is provident, and I suppose the opera-glass is to be used when the fish are rising."

Then the road led through wooded and watered valleys, whose bright colours and soft waving outlines were a pleasant contrast to the wildness and lonely grandeur of the higher hill-country. Before arriving at Bettws-y-coed (name loved of artists, and those to whom the windy woods of David Cox are pleasant memories), they halted near the Rhaidr-y-Wenol, and went down with the cameras to that fall, which lies deep in a wooded chasm, and even in dry weather well repays a visit. The darkness and moisture were unfavourable for photography, but the photographers were amply repaid by the spectacle of a tourist-party who were engaged in "doing the Swallow-fall." A clatter and clamour were heard on the hill-side, and suddenly three men were seen rushing down the hill-path with agitated faces, and at their topmost speed. They arrived at the bottom. They leapt like cats on the big stone which commands the falling water. They leapt off again as though the stone had been of hot iron. They rushed frantically up the hill-path, and were lost to sight. But they had "done the Swallow," and that was part of their day's programme, and therefore to be accomplished as rapidly and decisively as only Englishmen and Americans can accomplish such feats.

Beyond Bettws they trended to the right, and after twice crossing the Conway were soon careering along the valley of the Lledr, one of the most strikingly characteristic of all the Welsh valleys.

"Only see," said Caroline, "there are no less than four white umbrellas, each with an artist attached, in sight at this moment. They look at a distance like gigantic toad-stools, each with a leprechaun or its Welsh equivalent resting under the shade from the heat of the sun."

Jonas. "I wonder there are not more of them. See how gorgeously these feathered slopes of wood and fern and rock sweep down to the boulder-sown bed of the flashing Lledr, in whose runs and eddies (now mere rockpools) the great salmon live and leap when the autumn floods come down from the high mountains. And see how tenderly the distant outline of Siabod culminates in a far-off misty peak, closing and crowning a picture which no artist mind could ever forget."

Abraham. "By the way, talking of leprechauns and fairies generally, it is a strange thing that one has so few Welsh legends and superstitions on record, at least I know of but few and those of no unusual sort. One would have thought that every stony cwm and solitary mountain top, would have some haunting spirit of its own."

Jonas. "There are two very distinctive Welsh mountaineers' superstitions, which I remember to have seen in Mr. Will's Wanderings.*

---

* "A whole pack of hell-hounds are led on by their dark 'master,' a tall figure with a hunting pole, over

"First, there are the Cwn Annwn, or spirit-hounds, who are never seen of men, only their voices (like the deep baying of blood-hounds) are heard in stormy weather by the belated peasant on the mountain. The mountaineer believes too that when the voices seem to rise out of the mist at his very feet, the spirit-hounds are in truth hunting their prey in distant solitudes; when their baying is but faintly heard he goes on his way tremblingly, for then he knows that they are close upon him, perhaps even glaring in his white face with their glittering, wolfish, unseen eyes."

Abraham. "Wise men tell us that when we are most agitated by forebodings and prog-

---

the wastes of Dartmoor. . . The 'wish hounds,' as they are called in Devonshire, resemble in almost every particular certain 'spiritual hunting dogs' which are frequently seen and heard in the Principality; and of which a very curious account was published towards the end of the last century by 'the late Rev. Edmund Jones, of the Tranch, in Monmouthshire.'"—*Quarterly Review,* January 1861.

nostications of evil, the evil is in truth far distant: when evil comes, the warning thereof is commonly brief or disregarded."

Jonas (in lower tones). "Then there is the Cyoeraeth, the Hag of the Mist. Now, Caroline, listen and tremble. Her name means 'cold grief.' She sits in waste and lonely places on the mountains when the cold shroud of the night-fog is hanging over all. Her hair is matted and torn; she tosses her lank arms, clutching the dead stones with her crooked claws; she gnashes her black teeth, and flaps her leathern bats'-wings. Her face is the face of a corpse. Her wail freezes the life-blood of him who hears it. She swoops down from her hiding places towards the haunts of men. As she flies she drops from her outspread cloak those mighty boulders which cut into the torrent beds, and strew the hill-sides— stones which Abraham ignorantly calls 'blocs-perchés' and ascribes to glacier rather than to hag action. She shrieks, she flaps her wings against the window-pane of the lonely cottage, and moans the name of one within who dies surely and hopelessly before the rising of the dawn."

Caroline. "I really wish that you two would not indulge in this melancholy style of conversation. Between the moralizing of Abraham and the diablerie of Jonas, my life is fast becoming a burden to me."

Jonas. "Well then I'll make a diversion," and he sprung out of the car with his camera, and was quickly plunging among long fern and loose grass on the steep hill side below the road till he came to the bank of the Lledr, into which diminished stream he floundered and waded, and finally emerged triumphantly like a dripping water-god, having secured a stereogram of the lowest depths of the river's bed, a dry wilderness of confused rock and stone.

Higher up the valley another halt was made at Pont-y-pant, one of those aboriginal Welsh bridges of wood and stone, planks and piers, so characteristic of a primitive people.

"You see," said Jonas, "they thought it

better to build that which was easily built and easily repaired, than to raise a more costly structure which, comparatively speaking, would need no repair. A nation is becoming grey-headed before it discovers that capital spent on the permanent results of labour is capital laid out at a remunerating interest."

Still further on, almost at the head of the valley, they halted for the last time, at the terminus of their excursion, under the ruined walls of Dolwyddelan Castle, a square tower of grey stone springing up from a pile of fallen debris on an isolated mound at the foot of the swelling base of Moel Siabod. Here ensued high lunch, and grateful rest and shelter from the burning sunshine under the shadow of a great rock; and then more picture taking and more talk—a portion of which latter may here be quoted, and skipped by the reader if so he " ordain " as the Devonshire phrase has it.

Said Caroline, as she sat sketching the outline of Siabod, " I wish I could photograph, I don't think I would ever take the trouble of sketching again. I'd photograph the outline, and draw from that for all my water-colours. One gets so much more truth of outline in a photograph than in the cleverest of sketches."

Jonas went off at score, unfortunately perhaps set a-going on one of his hobbies.

"'What is truth,' Abraham?" he said, "even in such matters as outline? Caroline gives us hers, and my camera produces its truth, and your camera does what it can too —and all the results differ, as you may prove by rule and compass. Objective truth of outline is merely hypothetical, a conceivable idea, we know it to exist, but practically it is unattainable by man."

Abraham laughed. "Well, Jonas, you know I can't help that. I suppose you are going to be still more practical, and to urge that, in consequence, no man has a right to insist upon what he may call truth, because after all he can only prove that it is his truth or some one else's truth, not that it is truth independent."

Jonas. "Yes; I say a man has no right to

be dogmatic—no right to assert that his truth is exclusively true."

Abraham. " But what becomes of political speeches, scientific views, sermons, and the like ? A man can't be always hypothetical ; he must set up as a preacher of truth, if he preach at all."

Jonas. " He must preach his truth."

Abraham. " And allow that it is only his truth ?"

Jonas. " Can he prove it to be more? unless it be (which it may be, and is if it fructify) truth to some other mind or minds. No, he needn't say so. The thing is obvious to a thinking reader or listener, and those who don't think (generally the mass) would only be hopelessly bewildered by his assertions. Only, seeing that truth absolute and independent is the moral philosopher's stone, he will learn to be tolerant of other opinions ; he will preach his own truth (because that is every man's chief business in the world), but he will believe that some at any rate of those who preach doctrines which are not his may be preaching truth (*their* truth) also."

Abraham. " Still one truth may be truer than another, as one outline is more correct than another."

Jonas. " Granted; but how provable as such ?"

Abraham. " By a consensus, or by a majority of men."

Jonas. " In proving the truth of an outline we should try for a majority not of men, but of artist men."

Abraham. " Which accounts for the fact that truth is generally found to exist in the verdict of a minority ? "

Jonas laughed, and then mused; Caroline finished her sketch with rather a puzzled face.

Then they gathered up their cameras and other impediments, and there was a pleasant drive homewards through cool valleys and darkling woods, as the sun westered and sank and fell a burning globe of lurid fire beyond the distant misty mountain outline.

Some few days after this excursion, (which no traveller in Wales should omit, and which if an able-bodied pedestrian he may vary by crossing the mountain from Dolwyddelan to Pen-y-gwryd, visiting *en route* the lonely waters of Llyn Llynniaw,) Jonas proposed a visit to the great Menai Bridges. " We ought to add them to our list of stereograms," he said, "for each is in its way unique. And though we shall have to don our best bonnets and get into the civilized world again for a time, the change will do us good, and we shall return to the bosom of our first mountain love with renewed vigour and admiration."

Caroline. " Jonas to illustrate the power of affection appertaining to the superior sex, whose constancy lives and flourishes on change; and I to show a bright example of that womanly amiability and obedience in which Jonas doesn't believe."

Jonas. " Then you see we get, even before starting, a satirical speech out of Caroline; and I wish to get a critical speech from Abraham when the excursion is over."

Abraham. "I wonder if 'the Swell' would like to join us. I propose that we ask him; he is extremely amusing to me with his easy-going views of life, and he is perfectly gentlemanlike in his manner. In fact, whenever I look at him I can never help divesting him mentally of his travelling clothes, and seeing him with carefully brushed moustache and beard, dressed in the shiniest of tail-coats, the whitest of ties, and the tightest of gloves, leaning against the door post, or over the back of a crinoline-supporting chair, at one of those 'fashionable weunions' which afford him so evidently his congenial atmosphere."

Jonas. "Oh, don't ask him! He's a sort of thing I can't abide. Six months' hard labour at treadmill or crank-work would alone make him endurable, and teach him that life is not all Eau-de-Cologne and kid-gloves."

Caroline. "I beg to second Abey's motion. I think our Swell is extremely harmless, and that his conversation is an agreeable relief after the satire and severities of some other acquaintances of mine."

Exit Jonas in a spasm of disgust, and walks to Capel Curig and back in an hour-and-a-half, avowedly for the purpose of discovering whether there are any letters for him at the Post-office—which there are not.

But the trip was so arranged in spite of Jonas' opposition; and the party with the addition of "the Swell," (who urbanely accepted the invitation,) started early one fine and promising morning in Mr. Owen's largest car, with cameras and a duly-prepared stock of dry-plates. We will not describe the excursion, for is it not written in any and all of the guide-books with which Welsh towns are inundated during the season? And our story is only concerned with its close, which is here subjoined.

As they were driving home in the cool of the evening Jonas said, in the pause of an animated conversation which Caroline and her new companion were keeping up, "You have never told me, Abraham, what you think about the two bridges—relatively I mean. They present so great a contrast; something may be said about them."

"I think," said Abraham, "they chiefly remind me of the very obvious fact that decorative art (or rather beauty in art) lags slowly behind constructive art. What can be more beautiful than that fairy-like span of Telford's, with its gossamer threads and its graceful curves—how seeming light and fragile, and yet how strong and durable! Many suspension-bridges were built before these proportions were thought out. Then when the yet stronger and far grander fabric of Stephenson is thrown across the sea, how stiff and angular and rigid, how wholly inartistic is the result of his wonderful, and then almost unique, tube! Compare similarly the apparent unwieldiness and rigidity of the *Great Eastern* with the graceful beauty of some tiny yacht which hovers about its mighty mass; the garish regularity of the first Crystal Palace with the broken outlines and artistic effect of any old Cathedral; the hideosity of a locomotive with the quaint beauty of a Russian drotschy or a Canadian sledge. Time is the great beautifier after all, whether it works in the minds of men, or with its own artistic modeller's finger."

Jonas. "I wonder what Caroline says to your theory of the beautifying power of time!"

But that young woman was not listening to the above disquisition, edifying as she might have found it to be. She and "the Swell" were absorbed in their own conversation. During the whole of the day he had conspicuously attached himself to her; they had been chatting amicably on all manner of subjects; she evidently took a pleasure in drawing him out, and at length completely succeeded in awakening him from his partly assumed apathy. (She said afterwards that he really began to pronounce his r's.) He, in fact, was naturally roused by her natural ways and freshness of thought and fancy, so unlike the stereotyped routine of talk to which he had been accustomed in his own circle of society. And she feeling her power, exercised it the more freely on that account; and, perhaps, (we scarcely venture to hazard this perhaps,) because she saw that Jonas was obviously piqued at the interest she was taking in her fellow-traveller.

Jonas made many attempts to divert her attention from her companion. He was always stopping the car to gather a fern or a flower, which he was sure was something new and needed to have a consultation held upon it.

Abraham, unconsciously, aided and abetted Caroline by attempting to draw Jonas into a discussion of some abstruse point of photography. Jonas became fidgetty—then cross—then angry—then furious. At last, quite suddenly, he gave up his attempts to be agreeable—he threw his gathered ferns out of the car—lit a surly pipe, and smoked all the way home in silent dignity and most uncomfortable meditation.

CHAPTER X.

THE FRIEND IN NEED.

The rain came at last: after three months of scorching weather which had reduced every torrent to a scarcely visible brooklet, and narrowed every lake, and dried up the marshy lands, and seamed the parched surface of every morass, the long-expected change arrived.

Not as it comes in the lowlands, when a black canopy of rain-cloud is hung like a funeral vault over the whole country, when the winds are lulled and the rain falls heavily and monotonously and wearily from dark dawn to darker sundown.

"On the mountain" there is a strange bewildering activity of life, when the storm gathers, and the rain messengers are come.

At day-break the valley mists rise slowly and massively, pregnant with all the work to be done ere nightfall; rise slowly, clinging heavily to the mountain sides; rise slowly, and gather in dense squadrons around Snowdon and his satellite peaks. Over the green slope of Siabod peers a small white cloud "the size of a man's hand;" imperceptibly it waxes, and works upwards in the rising wind; now it is a margining fringe of lurid white along the whole range; now it spreads and joins the advanced guard on the Snowdon fortress. There is no wind now, only a still solemn deadly hush, as of a great army on the eve of battle.

There!—there is the signal of attack! A quivering line of pale-blue intense light zigzags across the scarp of Crib Goch; and then a hollow sudden boom far up in the mountains reverberates rolling from crag to crag with never-ceasing echo. Now a bright blaze leaps out of the blackening cloud-mass, and forks down on the very peak of Siabod; then a wild sweep of rattling hailstones follows, and a thunder crash shaking sky and mountain with its terrible utterance. Up the Gwynnant valley, and over the Llanberis watershed, a dense wall of whitest nimbus advances slowly; now it touches Pen-y-gwryd; now it is spread over the whole mountain district, wreathing itself in fantastic coils, breaking like spray against the grey boulders on the hill-side, opening out into sudden chasms and rifts— through which the distant mountains loom, already streaked with the white threads of new-born torrents.

Still the mountain artillery flashes and reverberates at uncertain intervals; and every now and then, through the rents of blinding drifting mist, and amid the increasing din of the elemental war, there flash out sudden phantasmagoric glimpses of calm cumuli sailing in the upper stratum of undisturbed air, and of the bright blue of the higher stormless sky.

It was a day of rest and idleness for the hard-working traveller.

"Let us light a big fire in Mrs. Owen's

saloon," said Abraham, "for this nor'-wester is shrewdly cold for all his many-voiced labours; and let us talk, and arrange our gatherings by flood and field, and make a batch of new flies, (for the streams will be down to-morrow, and the hungry fish will rise at last,) and, in fact, let us be as jolly as these very moist circumstances will allow."

Which was carried *nem. dis.* Jonas, however, being practically in a minority, for he shortly retired to one of the smaller sitting-rooms, in order (he said) to post up his diary, and write some letters of business.

In which retirement he lit a pipe, and planting his head stolidly on elbowed arms, mused misanthropically—misogamically too, on his prospects.

"Prospects!" he said bitterly, for the evil hour of distorted thought and untruthful hopelessness, which attacks us all, had arrived again for him,—"Prospects! Is it not enough that house, and fortune, and station should be taken away from me for no offence or fault of mine—that I should be condemned to a life-long sentence of counting-house imprisonment and mechanical hard-labour—and must this be added also ? This—that one, whom I believed to be above all the world as good and wise as she is beautiful, should prove to be light-of-heart, fickle-minded, carried away by the first handsome face of idle mindless vacuity which she encounters ?

"If I had told her I loved her with a love passing the love of women, she would have left me as she has left me now. No! There is no truth; nothing wise; nothing loveable. I will go home again. Home!" he added with inexpressible bitterness in his voice, "I will work in the dull round of daily, yearly duty till I grow grey-headed, and face-furrowed, till age comes, or sickness comes, or a speedy end comes more desired than aught besides. This I can do, and will do; but I will never love again, never hope again. I am old now : old, this day, for evermore. Would God I had never been young!

"What's that? what do you want?" he cried passionately, as the door opened and disclosed "Mary Ann," waitress, book-keeper, and what not, standing in the entrance with a scarcely repressed grin upon her face; she had heard voices, and had no idea of the benefit and necessity of a soliloquy.

"Please, sir, a car has just come in from Llanberis, and there is a gentleman, sir, come by it, who wants to see you, sir, immediate."

"See me? nonsense!" said Jonas, by no means yet recovered, "I don't know any gentleman from Llanberis; he must mean some one else. Shut the door will you and light this fire; it's confoundedly cold for summer in this horrid place."

"Oh, if you please, sir," replied Mary Ann immoveably, "the gentleman asked for Mr. White, and he's in the passage. This way please, sir," (turning round to the stranger,) "here's Mr. White, sir." And she ushered the visitor in, and closed the door after him, without paying the slightest regard to Jonas's dumb show of indignation.

The new arrival was a tall thin sallow-faced man of any age, with a care-worn expression about his eye, well-wrapped up in sundry waterproofs, which were dripping with the weather he had encountered.

"I believe I am speaking to Mr. Jonas White?" he said, in a slow hesitating voice.

"Yes," said Jonas, quite civilly and quietly, having mastered himself by a strong effort, "that is my name. Won't you sit down, and get off your wet things, and let me have this fire lit for you? The weather is not of a travelling sort to-day."

The stranger declined any alteration in the room or his dress, and sat down dreamily on a distant chair. Nothing was audible but the raving of the storm outside, and the drip and splash of the drenched traveller's garments within.

Jonas grew desperate again; it was hardly the day or the season for wet blankets. At length, with a greater effort at mastery than before, he said,

"May I ask whom I have the pleasure of addressing? Your face is not one that I can recall — perhaps you are mistaken in me; the name of White is not an uncommon one."

"Jonas White," said the stranger, sepulchrally, "is not a common name. Son of the late John Warnscombe White, merchant, of Ashburton Court, in the county of Essex. The same, I think?" as Jonas started with a gesture of surprise and uneasiness.

"Yes," he replied, "I am that man. Have you come to bring me any further addition to this day's darkness? I am accustomed to bad news; I shall bear it quietly."

"My name," said the stranger, after a seemingly endless pause, "is Carwithen. I live not far from Hawarden, where I saw your friend, Mr. Black, who gave me your address, and some account of you. Did he tell you he had seen me?"

"No," answered Jonas, wonderingly; "go on, if you please."

"Five-and-forty years ago," said Mr. Carwithen, "on this very day, nearly at this very hour, your father, John Warnscombe White, saved me from utter and fatal ruin, of body and mind, and station and name, and all that makes a man that which he is. I was a clerk in the house of which he was then junior partner; we had been friends at school and college; and his father was the senior partner of the firm. I had charge of a certain department of the firm's accounts. It happened one day in the usual course of events that my accounts were to be audited. They were audited, and there was a deficit—of no very large amount, but still a deficit of which there was no account. I was called into the presence of the firm, assembled in solemn conclave, and asked (kindly enough) to explain the discrepancy. I could not do so. I did not even know of the existence of the deficit; for I was naturally of a procrastinating turn of mind, and I had put off the balancing of my accounts from day to day, intending in truth that very morning to do it 'to-morrow'— which was a day too late, only one day too late for me. I muttered some incoherent sentence, burst into a torrent of tears, (I was a young man then,) and rushed away frantically to my lodgings. There I sat in dull hopeless torpor, thinking nothing, knowing nothing. When I had left the counting-house, your father (as I afterwards knew) began to plead for me. He urged my youth, my family, my character for honesty, and dilatoriness. Finally he prevailed so far as to be allowed to go in search of me, (it seems no one ever fancied for an instant that I should dream of escape,) and endeavour to get some rational explanation from me, if any such existed.

"He found me in my rooms, but I was then delirious; and there was a subsequent blank of many weeks filled only with the ravings of a brain fever and the weakness of recovery. At length when I could just crawl about my room he ventured to broach the subject again very quietly and tenderly.

"I knew nothing (except that I was not a wilful defaulter); I could remember no single circumstance which could in any way extenuate me. I gave him all my private accounts and papers and memoranda, and my office-desk key; and in my own office-room he worked hard after business hours for a week or more at the tangled web of public and private matters before him. I meanwhile only dimly conscious that my fate was hanging upon an invisible thread.

"One morning, (as it were this very morning, five-and-forty years ago,) he came into my bed-room, where I was sitting by a partly-opened window in the sunlight, dully counting the sparrows on the opposite roofs, and there was a quiet look of pleasure on his face which woke me up suddenly as from a long and disturbed dream.

"'What is it, John?' I said in a voice which I could not recognize for my own.

"'My dear Arthur,' he answered, 'you have been very foolish and very, careless, and you have had a near shave of it, but (now please don't excite yourself, you can't bear it,) you will do now. I have found out your mistake. The firm are quite satisfied, and on your written promise of far greater attention and precision for the time to come, will make no more allusion to what is happily past.'

P

"I believe I fainted then, in a quiet unconscious sort of way, and when I recovered, your father explained the nature of his discovery.

"He had gone over my accounts again and again with no favourable result; he had questioned (cautiously of course, for the matter was never made public,) the other clerks in my office in vain; he was on the point of renouncing the business in despair when a thought suddenly occurred to him.

"By night when I was wearily asleep he searched my rooms thoroughly—books, drawers, portfolios, bureau,—in vain. At length he came into my bed-room and searched my clothes quietly and systematically. In the pocket of the waistcoat I usually wore at the office there was a torn and crumpled piece of paper, almost illegible. This he carefully spread out and put together. It was a memorandum in my own handwriting that the sum of £50 received on account from a Mr. Taswell, a large city tradesman, had been paid by me (same day) on receipt of a cheque of Mr. Taswell's drawn on our firm and payable to Richard Williams, outfitter, Strand. I had duly debited myself with the £50, but had put off, till I had forgotten the circumstance, the entry of the payment. Still the paper was only a memorandum, and that in my own handwriting. Your father went in search of Mr. Williams, who most fortunately had drawn the money himself, perfectly recollected the circumstance, and produced his books to prove the receipt. So I was saved.

"The lesson was not thrown away upon me. My accounts were faultless thenceforth. I rose rapidly in the house, and in the estimation of my relations — which was of some consequence to me as the event proved.

"Many years afterwards an old bachelor-uncle of mine died and left me all his landed estates and funded property—more money than I could ever spend—because he said I was the only sensible hard-headed relation he had.

"Thereupon, after some consideration, I retired from the house; and in a final interview with your father before my departure I urged him, with all the arguments I could muster, to accept a lion's share of my windfall. I told him that I owed money, and good name, and life itself to him; that everything I possessed was rightly his. No, he would not take one farthing of what *was* his; he said he had enough, and more than enough for him. All my arguments and entreaties were in vain.

"At last he said, 'Well, Arthur, I'll tell you what you shall do. You say this money of yours is mine : of course it's not that, (he was always of a strict business turn of mind,) but, if you will, you shall promise me that if ever son of mine needs your help as you once needed help of me, you will help him as I helped you in your hour of need.'

"'So help me God, as I will so do,' I answered, and therewith we parted.

"I never saw him again.

"I let my estates in Staffordshire, and travelled for many years; circumstances of a purely individual nature, with which I will not now trouble you, having made a change of thought and life necessary for me. I was in South America when the panic ensued which killed my best friend. I heard of his ruin and his death simultaneously, or I need not say that all my wealth would have gone to reinstate him in his rightful position. He would not claim his own even in that last hour of want.

"Then I came home with a heavy heart, and sought out his son, according to my word.

"My experience of the father had taught me to be more cautious in attempting to help the son. But I would help you, and determined to do it without your knowledge and even against your consent. The money which your mother, and you too yourself, have received from year to year, came from me, in payment as I truly stated of a long-standing debt. Your situation, which now maintains you, was of my getting. I made interest for you, and arranged that in the course of time you should be taken into partnership, if you chose, by the house which you now serve.

"The other day your friend, Mr. Black,

confided to me some circumstances of your present life and future hopes—nay, don't be angry; (like his father! Just like his father!) he believed me to be a stranger to you, and your name was introduced by apparent chance into our conversation, and your story told as any other story of average interest might be told; and what he then said has induced a change in my plans. I must tell you that I am childless, and almost relationless; I have adopted my friend's son as my son. All my landed estates are entailed on you and your children—there are copies of the deeds.

"Upon your marriage, which I have now every reason to hope may shortly occur, I make you an allowance which I trust will suffice for your present wants—the details of which are in these papers which I shall leave in your hands.

"If you choose to adhere to your present line of life, I will arrange that you shall be taken into partnership by your house during the ensuing year. If you prefer a country life, come down with your wife and live with me at Evesbury. I shall be none the less happy when surrounded by cheerful and perhaps loving faces in my declining days.

"Now—do not answer me. Write to me in a week's time, or come to Evesbury yourself. Stay—no—write, in a week's time.

"I am going home at once. I came to-day, feeling that on this anniversary no distance or weather should hinder my rendering a tardy act of common justice."

Mr. Carwithen rose slowly from his chair; shook his dripping clothes; took Jonas' unresisting hand silently in his—and was gone.

Only the papers he had left on the inn-table, and the faint sound of the retreating car, persuaded Jonas that he was not waking from a dream.

"It *is* real," said Jonas, "yet after all it is too late. Only one day too late. I could not tell him that. Once before he was one day, only one day, too late."

"Oh, Caroline," he cried in the anguish of his heart, "yesterday I would have dared to ask you for that which would have been more than all the money in the world, to me;—to-day"—(in a lull of the wind the clear voice of Caroline and the deeper tones of a man's rejoinder were plainly audible as the door of their sitting-room was opened suddenly)—"to-day"—added Jonas with clenched teeth—"*never.*"

CHAPTER XI.

A NIGHT ON SNOWDON.

NEXT morning Pen-y-gwryd was itself again. Not a cloud dimmed the clear blue sky. The southerly wind was deliciously cool and fresh and fragrant. The once desolate voiceless mountain-sides were vocal with flashing, leaping, living torrents. The rapids on the Gwryd were roaring like a heavy ground-sea on a rocky coast. Every valley was full of light and life and music; and the kingly peak of Snowdon towered up into the calm sky, alone unaltered in the great new-birth of the natural world.

"My dear Jonas," said Caroline, as he came down to breakfast with pale face and haggard eyes at a late hour, "Abraham and I have just been proposing an excursion to the top of Snowdon; we think it will be a capital day for it, for the tourist tribe will be frightened by the state of the mountain roads, and we shall have his Majesty all to ourselves.

"What *is* the matter," she added, as she caught sight of his face for the first time, "what have you been doing to yourself? And please why did you go to bed last night in such a hurry, and never vouchsafe us an account of a mysterious stranger about whose odd ways Mary Ann is quite full this morning? She thinks he was not quite canny, and is rather afraid of you too, I believe.

"Oh, do tell me what is the matter, Jonas," she said again, laying her little white hand on his arm, "I can't bear to see you look like that."

"I am very sorry," said Jonas slowly, "that Miss Black should think it necessary to be at all anxious on my account," and thereupon feeling that he had committed himself, and was not at all prepared for an explanation, he left the room as suddenly as he had entered it.

Abraham looked at Caroline with a curious expression of amused enquiry about his face.

Caroline looked at Abraham with undisguised bewilderment in her eyes.

"Have you and Jonas been quarrelling, Abey?" she asked.

"No," he said, rather pointedly, "Jonas' quarrel is not with me."

"Oh, Abey," she answered, "how can you? You know I never quarrel with you, and wouldn't quarrel with your friends, if I knew how to do it—which I don't."

Abraham went on with his breakfast, merely observing that he thought the weather did not seem very favourable for Snowdon.

Caroline thought that a good cry would be a relief; and then she thought that it wouldn't; and then she went on with her breakfast.

How Jonas got *his* breakfast that morning is hitherto an unexplained mystery; probably he abstracted the necessary amount of oatcake from Mrs. Owen's reserves, washing it down with a friendly jug of porter on the kitchen settle. For, presently, as in that locality he was thus or otherwise employed, he heard a rattling of boxes and an evident excitement in the passage outside, towards which he turned with an air of abstraction and weariness, as though the whole world were stale and unprofitable and exacting, and he, Jonas, a living and lasting prey to its greed and rapacity.

To whom entered "the Swell" with the lightest of pocket siphonias over his arm.

"Good bye, my deah fellah," said that ingenuous young person, "I'm going in the caw with Hawwy Bach in thwee minutes. Just time to say adieu to you. Have alweady left my P.P.C. on your most agweeable fwiends."

"Going?" said Jonas, getting on his legs mechanically.

"Yes — weally. Pen-y-gaw-wed is thowoughly exhausted. Know evewy twee and shwub and wock in the neighbouwhood. Am going to hang out at the George, Bangoh Fewwy; was stwuck by the appeawance of that public. There was weally a miwwaw in the coffee-woom. Am tiwed of abowiginal life. Ta-ta."

And so saying he ascended, slowly and gravely, the car steps, and was soon whirled out of sight.

Jonas breathed more freely.

He strolled out into the little garden of the inn, and began to smoke.

By and bye Caroline came up to him with her hat in her hand, and a half conscious flush on her cheek.

"Please to tell me, Jonas," she said, quite softly and humbly, "what I have done to offend you. I am very sorry."

Jonas was utterly taken aback by this line of tactics; there was, in fact, no answer of a rational kind left open to him. Evidently she had a right to talk to the now-departed "Swell" if she preferred his conversation to Jonas and his exigence. What could he say?

At last he muttered something about a

headache; and for the first time in his life wished that Caroline would go away, which that young woman had no intention of doing.

She said rather sorrowfully, "Why am I to be Caroline one day, and Miss Black the next?" and then with a mischievous smile, "Come in now, and be good, and I'll give you some breakfast."

Jonas began to be afraid that the point of dispute would be glossed over after all; and so he said abruptly,

"Do you know that your friend 'the Swell' has just gone to Bangor? Shall we make an excursion to-day in that direction?"

Caroline flushed up. "Jonas, you have no right to talk to me in that way. What have I said or done to justify you? You are a man, and I am not. It's quite cowardly of you." And the tears began to stand in her eyes.

Jonas thawed at once.

"I am very sorry," he said, "I did not mean to be rude or unkind to you."

She took her advantage.

"Yes, Jonas, you did indeed. Because I

took pity on that very harmless young gentleman, and listened to his London-made prattle, and was civil to him, and smoothed down Abraham's polite contempt, and your brusqueness, you chose to quarrel with me, and make hard speeches to me. And I never said an unkind word to you, or thought an unkind thought of you in my life. Is that fair to me?"

Jonas melted; his self-tormentor vanished in an instant; he saw only his own folly and hardness; he held out his hand and said,

"Will you forgive me? I have been very foolish, and very rude, and very unkind. It is all my fault. I always was a brute—will you forgive me, this once; and let me call you Caroline again?"

Caroline took his hand, and said nothing.

Jonas felt a strange huskiness in his throat.

A few words were welling up from his heart, but they did not break out into articulate utterance.

After all the wayside garden of an inn is hardly the place for "utterances."

Then Abraham came in, not inopportunely

on the whole; and seeing the attitude of reconciliation, rejoiced.

"Now," he cried cheerily, "let us go and do Snowdon. The day is young and promising. Come Jonas! come Caroline!—hats, alpenstocks, cameras, and what not!"

"When shall we start?" asked Caroline, recovering her voice, "and how are we to go, Abey?"

"Oh, we'll have a pony for you, and Jonas and I will walk, and Mr. Owen shall go too, and take care of the pony and carry your shawls and wraps."

"No," said Caroline, "that 'll never do. If I can scramble up Twll-du, and all along the sides of Llanberis Pass, I can surely walk up Snowdon. Now I'll tell you my plan. You shall be guide; you know every path on the mountain. You shall take up your camera with you; Jonas shall carry my cloak and fern-box: and we'll be independent of ponies and guides and every other sort of impediment."

Jonas in his penitence would have carried

Caroline to the peak and back again if she would have let him, and said so. And then there were speedy preparations, and a filling of flasks, and a packing up of provisions in a spare botanical tin; and, as they were about to start, Mr. Owen appeared and offered them a cast as far as Pen Pass in a car which he was going to drive to Llanberis—an offer which was accepted with many thanks—and so they set off none the less happy that the storms physical and moral had cleared off into such bright and cheerful sunshine.

There was small fatigue in walking along the level path on that fresh morning, and the sun as yet had but little power, and they were soon skirting the shores of Llyddaw.

"Here we are," said Jonas, "already 1800 feet above the sea-level in the midst of an old glacier valley. I needn't point out to our now instructed eyes all the signs of old-world action. Only I must quote Professor Ramsay once more, because he seems to love this valley with all his heart, as I do. 'Around it,' he says, as I remember—stay—here is my

note-book, and here are his very words—
'around it rise the cliffs of Lliwed, Crib Goch, and Pen Wyddfa, seamed with veins of white quartz looking like streaks of snow on the tall black rocks that circle the vast amphitheatre, the scarred sides and rugged outlines of which sharply defined against the sky, may well seem, till attempted, hopelessly inaccessible to the unpractised climber. In every season and phase of weather there is a charm in this valley to the lover of the mountains. In quiet sunshine, when the rocks—and perhaps a lazy ferry-boat—are reflected in the still water; or while the wanderer scales the crags amid the seething mists; or when the pitiless rain or hail or snow comes driving down the valley; but, best of all, in a threatening evening, when the gathered clouds, like the roof of a vast cavern, hang heavily from side to side on the edges of the hills, and a streak of light caught from the setting sun shows redly behind the dim peak of Snowdon, grimly reflected in the sombre waters of the lake.'

"That is good," added Jonas, "I always

copy a heartily-written description when I can get hold of one, it teaches one to see as well as to write."

In half-an-hour more they were on the shores of Glassllyn, whose marvellously-blue waters, rippling under the central Snowdon peak, shone out like a sapphire in a setting of ebony.

"Now comes the real work—an hour's pull, and a hard pull," said Abraham, as he began the zig-zag ascent leading up the side of the mountain.

"When Caroline is tired," he added, "I will show you how we will help her almost as much as a pony would."

And by-and-bye as she flagged in spite of her untiring spirit, he and Jonas held either end of her alpenstock, and placing her between them, carried a moving handrail for her up the steep and stony path, which speedily enabled her to reach the higher ridge without a stumble and with but small fatigue.

Here they threw themselves down on the

short grass to rest, and examine the panorama which was beginning to open out before them, tracing their path to the exit of Llyddaw, and speculating on the terrors of a winter's ascent when the driving snow was hiding the rugged track, and an easterly gale hurrying the blinding hailstones across the desolate mountain wastes.

Then there was a vast scrambling search for flowers and ferns, for which on the way up Jonas had made many a discursive ramble, and the results whereof and of the day generally, viewed in a botanical light, he afterwards chronicled in a note here subjoined.*

---

* Obvious Snowdon flora.—J.W.—July and August.
    Triglochin palustre,
    Saussurea alpina,
    Subularia aquatica,
    Saxifraga hypnoides,
    ———— stellaris,
    ———— cæspitosa,
    ———— nivalis,
    Chrysosplenium oppositifolium,

Abraham meanwhile secured a stereogram of the summit from a point in the ridge which is common to the two ascents from Capel Curig and Llanberis; and then a ten minutes' walk landed them on the highest peak of the great Carnarvonshire range, some 3,500 feet above the level of the visible sea.

"It's a grand old mountain, Caroline," said Jonas, "in spite of its high roads and rival

Trollius europeaus, ⎫
Mecanopsis cambrica, ⎬ not in flower.
Thalictrum alpinum, ⎭
Cochlearia officinalis,
——— anglica,
Rhodiola rosea,
Armeria maritima,
Oxyria renifornis,
Silene acaulis, near the peak,
Juncus squamosus,
Epilobium alpinum,
——— alternifolium,
Polypodium dryopteris,
Scolopendrium vulgare,
Cystopteris fragilis,
Asplenium viride,
Woodsia ilvensis.

hotels on the consecrated ground of the wind-torn peak. Look at the lakes below, twenty—thirty shall we say? More than a score of sparkling diamond points of light scattered about on the heaving bosoms of the wide hill-country. There is Llanberis down in the mist—and there is Carnarvon—and the low hills of Anglesea—and there, far beyond the purple sea-line where the clouds are gathering silently, are the Irish mountains—beyond whose jagged outlines the westering sun will sink to-night, when his work of love is ended."

Caroline. "It is all far more glorious and thrilling than I could have dreamt of. I would not have missed this great panorama for worlds; I see now the truth of what Abey said about panoramic views."

Abraham. "After all one does not wonder that Alpine and Pyrenean travellers can return to the Carnarvonshire mountains, and find that their early admiration and affection are in no way abated. One feels instinctively that Wales has all the essentials of a mountain land; and that it is so, the traces of the old snow would abundantly prove. That Welsh mountains are smaller than Alpine mountains does not argue their inferiority to my mind. We can recognize proportion and uniformity of plan and purpose as well here as in all other mountain countries."

Caroline. "And after all you have told me I can bring back in fancy the old world of snow and glacier as clearly as though it were now around us."

Jonas. "And perhaps feel less chilly and on the whole more jolly than if you were perched on the topmost ridge of an eternal snow-peak in a blue veil and gogglers—which would not be becoming even to you, Caroline."

And there they sat absorbing quietly the great view detail by detail, watching the shadows wandering up the distant passes, and the many-twinkling lakes fade away one by one as the sun fell, like stars paling at early dawn. Many hours were so spent happily, and at length Abraham roused himself from a far-off reverie, and in his capacity of guide said that they must think of moving homewards.

"See," he added, "there is a sudden mist-bank wandering up from the southward. I have been watching it rise from Teyern and Llyddaw, and now Glassllyn is partially obscured. We must go. I know the path stone by stone, but if we are belated, and a heavy fog should ensue, I would not answer for my powers of getting you down safely."

"Oh," said Jonas, "there is plenty of time yet. The sun is still shining out there; and we ought to patronize one of these rival hotel-establishments before we go."

So they entered one of the huts, and refilled their flasks, and chatted with the proprietor, and might have stayed longer, but that Abraham, whose mind was not easy on the subject of the fog-bank, got up and looked out, and peremptorily ordered a start.

"There are some heavy clouds hanging about," he said, "and the fog is decidedly increasing. Come, Caroline! come, Jonas! Once get down to Glassllyn, and I don't care how long you loiter on the road—but there is really now no time to lose."

Whereupon a start was effected promptly —and not before it was time.

On leaving the ridge of Wyddfa and commencing the descent to Glassllyn, they saw that a very dense sea of black fog was slowly climbing the mountain, while overhead the cumulus was gradually lowering to meet it.

Abraham got fidgetty, but said nothing.

In ten minutes they were enveloped in the mist, which was driving slowly before the wind. Though they could only see a few feet before them, it was evident that the sun was below the horizon, for the darkness increased momentarily.

In a very few minutes more the path was only visible at their feet; the mist drifted more and more heavily, and night seemed to have set in without warning.

Caroline was wrapped up in her warm cloak, and placed between Jonas and Abraham, holding the alpenstock as before.

"I hope you're a good guide," said she to Abraham.

"Well," he answered, "I must do my best,

but I didn't bargain for this. The sudden turns of the path are bewildering enough in this sort of weather."

By-and-bye he stopped, and pulled a coil of thin rope out of his pocket.

"I generally carry this," he said, "it's useful in many ways, and now we shall want it. I don't feel quite sure about this turn. Here, Jonas, you hold on to one end of the line, and I will go out into the fog with the other and reconnoitre; it won't answer to part company, which we might very easily do."

Presently he was again visible, but not till he could have touched Caroline with his outstretched arm, and then he said, "I think we are right; now let us tie ourselves together in a string, and then a false step won't do any material mischief."

The fog thickened every instant, and drifted heavily, and the darkness became intense—hopelessly so at last. After a quarter of an hour's blind stumbling there was a pause as if by common consent.

"Whereabouts are we?" asked Caroline, who greatly enjoyed the excitement.

Abraham. "I haven't the very faintest idea. We are going down hill, but where we are going, and whereabouts Glassllyn lies, I can't pretend to tell you. One thing is quite obvious, that we've lost the path; and another thing is probable, that we shall not find it again till a little more light is thrown upon the subject."

Jonas. "Oh, we've only got to go on down hill; we must get into the valley road at last."

"Yes," said Abraham, "that's true enough; but as we can't see a foot before us, it is quite evident that one false step might take us over the sliding face of some hidden scarp, or plunge us heels over head in a floundering bog. This won't do. One plan only is left; we must untie ourselves again, Jonas shall take the alpenstock and lead Caroline thereby, and I will go forward short stages with the line as far as the tether will let me; so, having made sure of the ground, you can follow in safety."

For half-an-hour they worked on in this fashion, very slowly of course. At length on one of Abraham's pilot excursions a sharp cry was heard and Jonas felt the line tighten. He held on, and shouted.

"All right!" cried Abraham, "stay where you are. There's no damage done. I shall get out directly." And presently he appeared in a somewhat deplorable condition, having been suddenly soused nearly up to his waist in a hidden bog, and having twisted one ancle in his struggles.

"What *are* we to do?" asked Caroline anxiously, beginning to wish that the excitement was well over.

"There's only one thing to be done," said Abraham, "it's no use to go in this blind and helpless fashion; we shall only get into worse scrapes than this. We must make up our minds to camp out for the night. I've done it before, and it's not unpleasant, when done properly. Now let's consider. It will be daylight about four o'clock, there are not more than six or seven hours to provide for. A very few minutes ago we passed under the lee of a great rock; I propose that we go back and try to find it again; it will give us all the shelter we can possibly require."

"Well," said Jonas, "personally I can sleep under a rock as well as any man; but what does Caroline say to the arrangement?"

"Oh, I shall enjoy it immensely," she answered with a laugh, "and anything is better than floundering about all night long in a wet fog."

After some difficulty the desired rock was found. It proved to be a projecting mass of hard stone, composed of three or four huge weather-worn rocks, which had apparently fallen from the mountain above; and afforded several very available sheltering places.

"Why—here's almost a cavern!" said Jonas, as he scrambled into a deep niche, "and it's quite dry underneath, and quite warm; we shall do capitally! And here's a lot of dry grass and fern; some of which will make no end of a carpet, and with the rest we'll make a blaze just to see the extent of our hotel."

The fire, which burnt up for a minute and then died out again, served to show them that there were no precipices or morasses in their immediate neighbourhood, and that with a little management they might weather out the night in safety and even in comfort.

So Jonas wrapped up Caroline carefully, and placed her on a soft cushion of grass at the further end of the niche, and then he and Abraham curled up their legs and fitted into the entrance.

"Now," said Caroline, "that's what I call comfortable. I vote that in the next place we order up our supper."

"Supper!" said Abraham, rather dolefully, as he was scraping the mud off his boots, "not much hope of that I fancy till to-morrow, at all events."

"Why," answered Caroline, cheerily, "you don't half know the resources of our larder. Jonas has got my spare tin quite full of sandwiches, and big ones too, which no one has thought about—and I put half-a-dozen thick biscuits into my bag on the top of Snowdon, thinking that they would do to devour on the way down. And Jonas has got a flask full of brandy, and so have you, Abey. What more can mortal man or woman desire?"

Abraham began to cheer up.

"And," said Jonas, "I've got a reserve of tobacco, and plenty of lights. On the whole I fancy we shan't much miss Pen-y-gwryd to-night."

So there was high supper; and they found it to be a very warming and invigorating proceeding.

"We must have some water for the brandy," said Jonas,—"stay—I think I hear a trickling not far off. It may be only the dripping from the mist; but let me have the end of the tether, and I'll go and see."

Presently he returned with his flask cup full of clear water, and reported the existence of a flourishing runlet in the vicinity. Several other excursions of the same nature served to provide brandy-and-water, ("very much *with-*

out," said Jonas,) for the whole party. Then there was a quiet consumption of tobacco, and much speculation as to Mrs. Owen's probable anxiety about her truant guests.

At last Abraham announced his intention of sleeping till day-break, and advised his companions to follow his example, which he began to carry out by wrapping a corner of Caroline's cloak round him and coiling himself up in as comfortable a position as circumstances would allow. Presently his low and regular breathing announced his final success.

Jonas leant back against the sides of the rock, and thought he would go to sleep too.

Caroline, just visible at arm's length from him, was quite quiet, and probably was following her brother's wise example.

Outside their little room, now warm and perfectly sheltered, the wind was moaning fitfully and the mist driving by in heavy black masses.

But Jonas could not sleep, try as he would.

He lit another pipe, and smoked it out, and tried again.

First, a tall gaunt figure, with careworn haggard eyes, stood before him in the gateway of the mist, promising in sepulchral tones untold wealth and endless summer days of happiness; and then the wind rose and howled, and the mist broke out complainingly into plashing weltering rain.

Then, there came up a bright sunny vision of the old home country-house, with its stately avenues of fragrant limes, and cheerful welcoming voices in the great buttressed porch after adventurous wanderings, not all unprolific, in search of bird and beast and plant and rock—the future denizens of the great museum which it was then the greatest ambition of the vision-seer to found.

Afterwards, a shadowy gleam of yellow fog which dimly discoloured one asthmatic sparrow sitting all alone on all manner of London house-tops, and peering dreamily into a well-known and dingiest apartment decorated with ricketty round-bottomed stools, and ink-besmirched, hard-angled desks, and stiff-backed ledgers which no amount of labour would ever add up.

Jonas was plainly beginning to doze. He turned uneasily, and roused suddenly with a start, thinking that he heard a voice which he well knew call him by name.

He sat up, and looked—as far as he could in the dense fog—and listened.

Abraham's regular breathing beat like the pendulum of the great Westminster clock. Caroline was still, motionless, a grey wraith framed in a grey mist-wreath.

Jonas struck a fuzee and looked at his watch, and then hastily filling his pipe lit it with the dying ember.

"Jonas!" said Caroline, stirring in her sleep.

Jonas leant forward, and stretched out a hand in the darkness.

There were two hands that touched.

Abraham slept well.

"Caroline!" said Jonas.

The hands were not loosed.

"Caroline!" said Jonas again, quite quietly, the words coming to him of their own accord, "will you care for me who care for you more than for all the world besides?"

Caroline seemed to stir again in her quiet sleep; was she dreaming? was she awake?

"Jonas!" she said dreamily.

"Caroline," he said again, and this time it was no dream, for his hand left no uncertain touch when his heart went out in its grasp, "Caroline, will you love me who love you more than all the world?"

The wind outside howled and raved, and the mist drove by blindingly.

Caroline's dream was over.

She drew back her hand shrinkingly, and wrapped herself more closely in her cloak, with a slight mechanical shiver.

Should she wake Abraham?

She looked out into the dark wild night. Then she said,

"Jonas, don't you think you are dreaming in your half sleep, as I—as I was just now when you wakened me?"

"Yes," answered he, "dreaming as I dream always, waking or sleeping. Oh, Caroline, tell me that you care for me! I cannot live without your love; give it me now before it is too late—give it me who have never deserved it—give it me who hunger and thirst for it with my whole heart and my whole soul!"

"My dear Jonas," said Caroline, thoroughly aroused by his passionate words, and with a spark of her own humour stirred up in her, "how can you go on in that wild way? Why you are as bad as the weather! Supposing I could 'care' ever so much for such an exigeant as you, what would be the use of it?"

Jonas groaned.

She put out her little soft hand to him again.

"Please will you be practical?" she said, "you know that I know all about you and your prospects in the world."

"Prospects!" ground he out between set teeth.

"Now, Jonas, do be reasonably quiet. How could I ever consent to be an additional burden to you and those for whom you work so hard and so carefully? If I cared for you, *could* I do so?"

And then her voice broke.

The rain swept by, and the wind wandered wearily in far-off hidden valleys.

"Caroline," he said, "I would work for you as I never worked before, or could work before. Only tell me that I may hope. Tell me that nothing but the bitter want of money which should be mine, which may be mine some day, can ever part our love. Tell me this—tell me that you care for me, all unworthy as I am of your forgiveness and your love."

He half rose as he spoke. Her hand clung instinctively to his; she drew it gently to her lips; she said,

"Jonas, I have nothing to forgive; I will love you if you will let me."

Then by her side, with one protecting arm round her who nestled happily in that strong shelter, heedless of driving mist and wailing night, he told her—listening to him with a new-growing feeling of strange dreamy bewilderment—all the story of the yesterday; how that he had climbed suddenly from poverty to wealth; that there was enough and to spare, now, for all who cared for him; that he had loved her long and earnestly, too *really* ever to ask her to share his need as now he asked her to crown his happiness.

"And so you wouldn't trust me, dear Jonas?" she said, half reproachfully; and yet perhaps she loved him all the more for his quiet self-denial, unusual in men's natures, and most of all in natures of men like Jonas.

"And you really took me in; and made me say that I would wait for you goodness knows how long—perhaps till you were quite grey-headed, or bald-headed, and unable to sit comfortably on anything but a hard three-legged stool! Mind, sir, this is the last—the very last time, that you behave to me in this deceitful way! I will forgive you only this once——and not now if you——Jonas!"

The rest of which speech was totally inaudible, for some unexplained reason.

However, Abraham was unaccountably disturbed as a corollary: he rolled over, uncoiled himself, rubbed his eyes, and then gave utterance to the following formula, which, as far as our experience goes, is invariable in the case of suddenly-awakened men,

"Hullo—yes—all right—what's o'clock?"

Jonas sat upright, and lit a fusee.

"Three thirty-five," he said. "Why, you've had a long nap, Abraham."

"Ah! yes!" said that very unconscious person, "always sleep well. Half-past three? Oh!—there," (attempting to get up, and knocking his head against the rock in consequence,) "confound the rock! Let's have a look at the weather," and he turned out. "Why, it's really clearing: not half so much mist; there's something like a star. Why, it'll be daybreak directly. Caroline awake?"

"Yes," said Caroline, demurely, "I've been awake for some little time."

"Well, let's have breakfast; brandy-and-water and a biscuit; we shall see our way out of this wilderness in half-an-hour, and no bad thing either, for I'm terribly stiff in the legs."

Which repast was finished, and then they stood together at the mouth of their resting place, watching the mist melt away very gradually as the cold shimmering dawn slipt over the hidden hills.

Caroline touched Jonas' hand. He understood her by some strange new-born sympathy, and took her hand in his, and said to Abraham in quite an ordinary voice,

"This is my property now."

"Eh?" said Abraham, not at all knowing what was the article alluded to. "What's your property?"

"This," said Jonas.

Then the story had to be repeated, interrupted by Abraham's exclamations of surprise and joy; and then the sun rose with a sudden flash of amber light, flooding the awakened valleys, breaking against the stony mountain crests, and dissipating the still wavering wreaths of clinging mist—just as the last few hours of the night had driven away the denser clouds of heavy-hearted hope, and heralded the dawn of a sunny and cloudless future.

"Bravo!" said Abraham, as the light became strong and clear, "not such very bad steering after all! Where do you think we really are? Why, there's Glassllyn a mile behind us, and there's Llyddaw and Teyern just under us. We never got half as much down hill as we fancied. We kept very much in the track of the old road from Pen Pass; and here we are half way up the mountain, and—yes, it was very lucky we stayed where we are. That is by no means a cheerful bog, nor is that an agreeable precipice below us! Now, let us keep along this shoulder, and we shall be on the Llanberis watershed in half-an-hour. Right shoulders forward! March!"

And in an hour's time a very happy and merry party arrived at Pen-y-gwryd, and roused the still sleeping household, who had given up the errant travellers at nightfall, thinking that they had followed the not-uncommon example of many tourists, and had slept at the "Snowdon Hotel," in the hope of a cloudless sunrise in the mórning.

"Slept under Crib Goch, ma'am!" said Mrs. Owen, with endless surprise, "and indeed you must be cold enough now, and want your breakfast bad enough, and indeed you must!"

And indeed the breakfast No. 2 was by no means unacceptable.

CHAPTER XII.

HOMEWARDS AND HOME.

PEN-Y-GWRYD seemed to have lost all its charms for Jonas. The Glyders were a bore. He could not fish for half-an-hour consecutively, even though Caroline carried his basket, and the fish rose freely. She complained that he had never found a fresh fern since the memorable night on Snowdon.

Abraham told him that he was worse than useless in the photographing room, for he couldn't even weigh out six grains of pyrogallic without making a blunder.

In fact, he had set his face stedfastly towards Devonshire; and when the week was out, and he had written a letter to Mr. Carwithen, full of grateful thanks and happy plans for the future, and another to his mother (who consumed many days in rightly taking in its contents), he never rested till "Judy" was packed up and forwarded by coach and luggage train, and the whole party were safely *en route* for Llangollen-road station.

They bade farewell to Pen-y-gwryd with much regret after all, and quite overwhelmed Mr. and Mrs. Owen with their hearty acknowledgments of all the kindness and attention which had been shown to them.

Jonas inscribed names and dates in the visitors' book on their departure, and added the ensuing composition, which Caroline leaning over his shoulder followed word by word, as he copied it out of his tattered note-book.

" Pen-y-gwryd, Pen-y-gwryd,
  High away among the mountains,
  High away in breezy cloudland;
  Haunted by all changeful shadows
  When the summer sunsets linger
  Opalescent on the Glyders,
  Bathing all their crags in glory,
  Making earth one great sky-portal;

Roused to stern and wrathful grandeur
When the wild and rushing storm-wind
Howling in the wildernesses,
All the 'cold grey stones' of Snowdon,
Sweeps across the reeking moorland,
Pipes away to Capel Curig,
Riots o'er the seething waters,
Trumpeting in hidden passes,
Lost in crag, and cloud, and distance.

" Far it is from haunts of tourists
Trim-kept, clad in gorgeous garments,
Borne in cars across the mountains,
Loving coffee-rooms and waiters,
Lisping lazily of comfort,
Babbling beerily of bar-maids,
' Doing Snowdon!' 'doing Cader!'
Hurrying home to desk and counter,
Ignorant of one emotion
Raising hearts from mountain skywards.

" One, we well remember, wandered
Up the pass to Pen-y-gwryd,
Redolent of Regent Street, he
Bore an opera-glass depending
Shinily from well-drest shoulders,
Lisping faintly, ' Clevaw people
Come, they say, to Pen-y-gaw-wed,'
Wisely went his way rejoicing.

" Let it be so, landlord, ever!
Best of landlords, Henry Owen,

Best of guides on moor and mountain
When the fog-banks gather grimly
Round impenetrable passes,
Guard thine inn of Pen-y-gwryd
(Happiest of resting-places,
When the world is making havoc
With a soul that seeks but quiet,
'Calm delights,' and loving duty,)
Guard thine inn of Pen-y-gwryd
From the well-bred idler-tourist;
Only let thy roof-tree shelter
Him who loveth nature truly;
Him who findeth on the mountain
Summer calm in wintry weather;
Him for whom the Heavens open
Rifts of blue in every storm-cloud;
Him to whom earth preacheth gladness,
Workful rest and adoration."

Caroline. "Now, Jonas, I've got a great mind to tear that leaf out of the book, and I would if it wasn't for Mr. Owen's sake. Mind that is the last allusion of the kind you make about my friend, 'the Swell!' I think he is a very laudable young person, and I won't have him called names."

Jonas leant back in his chair, and Abraham walked discreetly out of the room and ordered the car round; and then there was fresh leave-taking and a practical end of the happily terminated experiences in North Wales.

We need not follow them too closely as they lingered for a day or two at Shrewsbury, beguiled by its quaint old, black-and-white chequered, gable-ended, timber-built, Elizabethan houses; or as they loitered in the shady Cathedral green of quiet Hereford; or wandered in the dim cloisters of garish Gloucester.

A rapid passage down channel in the easy-going "Juno" landed them again on the pier at Ilfracombe; and then a day's journey brought them to their journey's end.

"Always glad to see dear old Marscombe," said Abraham throwing himself down luxuriously in his own arm-chair. "By the way, when are you going away again, Caroline?" he added mischievously.

Caroline flushed and ran up-stairs, "to look after the luggage" she said.

But in a month's time, or thereabouts, the Marscombe bells were ringing merrily, and there was a great feast given by Abraham to all his tenants and half the country round; and the health of Mr. and Mrs. Jonas White was received rapturously, and with all conceivable and inconceivable honours.

Jonas and Caroline set out on their wedding tour, halting *en route* in London, where Mrs. White and her daughters were staying in their old lodgings.

"My dear," said that excellent matron, having duly kissed and praised Caroline, and told Jonas that she thought far more of his getting a good wife than of his sudden accession of fortune—a speech which delighted him almost as much as the memorable oration of Mr. Carwithen—"My dear, what do you think that very mysterious and kind-hearted Mr. Carwithen has done for us?"

"Upon my word," answered the radiant Jonas, "it's quite impossible to say. Probably he has made you a present of a diamond mine, and bestowed upon Annie an extensive tract in the gold-digging country. He is extremely like a good enchanter in a fairy story; he appears at the nick of time, and makes everybody jolly whether they will or no. Indeed, if I didn't see Caroline before my waking eyes I should think I was the victim of magic, and expect to wake up to the familiar darkness of the old office-life again; but after all truth is stranger than fiction. Well, mother, and what has Mr. Carwithen been and done? You know he has already given me enough for everybody."

"Oh," said Mrs. White, "indeed, he's not contented with that; here is his own letter. Annie and I are quite independent once more, thank God! and there will be no more anxiety about the Christmas bills, and no more hard work for you, dear Jonas—best and kindest of sons that you have always been to me."

"Well," said Jonas, having read Mr. Carwithen's brief communication with very bright eyes, "and what did you answer?"

"Answer?" said Mrs. White slowly, "now I really can't tell you. I know I filled six sheets of letter paper and crossed them all

s

over twice, and then Miss Annie was pert enough to say that she couldn't make head or tail of my labours, and I believe wrote him a little note herself. I'm sure your father's bread has come back to his own fifty-fold, after wanderings in many waters; and I think I mentioned that in my letter."

Jonas and Caroline travelled through the Alps, and then went down to the Pyrenees and wintered happily at Pau. How Caroline was delighted with these new scenes we may not stay to tell, but she always said that, of all mountains she loved Snowdon the best.

In the ensuing spring they returned to England, and settled down calmly to a quiet country life at Evesbury; near which place Mrs. White and Annie were already installed in a pretty cottage, by Mr. Carwithen's forethought.

He was an altered man from the day of his new children's arrival; no longer a melancholy recluse, he became a bright, cheerful, active-minded man; and when grey hairs came at last, he said that their chiefest honour and crown were the happy faces and ringing laughter of his little grandchildren, who were always clambering about his knees, and tottering after him in his daily walks.

Not long after their establishment at Evesbury, Caroline received a characteristic letter from Abraham, which was the last drop required to fill her cup of peace.

"You will be glad to hear, dearest Caroline," he wrote, "that I am going to make a slight alteration in my Marscombe life.

"I wrote a few lines the other day to your old friend, Amy Lee, and enclosed a note for the squire, which she was to burn or deliver as she willed.

"He answered me; and she didn't.

"And now I am going to Hawarden in a few days; and shall pay you a visit on that occasion.

"I have no doubt that I shall be managed by Amy as, successfully (and uncomplainingly on my part) as I was by Caroline; and I trust that you will shortly receive a notice to the following purport:—

"'Marscombe Cottage, chief superintendent and general comptroller, Amy Black *vice* Caroline White recently promoted.'

"Kindest remembrances to Jonas, who I have no doubt is as efficient a subordinate as you can desire."

At the following Christmas there was a great family gathering at Evesbury Hall, and thereat Jonas found himself making an after-dinner speech, which eventuated in becoming chiefly biographical and retrospective, and was at length checked by the tears of his mother and the interruption of Mr. Carwithen, who ever refused to hear any allusion which might be made to his own share in the happiness of his friends.

But these were Jonas's concluding sentences.

"There are few brighter examples," he said, "than that which our own happy and united family affords of the fact that no kind and self-denying action will ever lose its reward. The reward (shall I say testimonial rather than reward, or equivalent ?) will come sooner or later; perhaps in life—as our friend Mr. Carwithen has told us, in his goodness, that it has come to him already; if not, it comes afterwards, and his friend, my father, knows now that I speak truth for him and in his name.

"And once more, for at Christmas-time these thoughts are not misplaced—I believe too that no human life of sorrow is in the end uncomforted, no hearty labour is uncrowned, no faith exists which does not find fruition, no weather howsoever stormy which does not tend hourly to its final calm.

"I drink now to the memory of the darkest hours of my life, because they were the birth-place and the cradle of the restful peace which now, of God's mercy, I enjoy.

"Here comes the good old Wassail Bowl, and now drain a bumper to bygone days; and a health to all who, like ourselves, have been storm-vexed, weather-beaten pilgrims in life—night-belated travellers waiting hopefully for God's own hour of daybreak,

'On the Mountain.'"

THE END.

www.ingramcontent.com/pod-product-compliance
Lightning Source LLC
Chambersburg PA
CBHW031950230426
43672CB00010B/2117